90
Instructional
Strategies
For the Classroom

By

Janet Aaker Smith

Pieces of Learning

© 2006 Pieces of Learning
CLC0401
ISBN 1-931334-90-0

90 Instructional Strategies

1. A-Z Lists
2. Acrostic Facts
3. Add a Letter
4. Add a Word
5. Alpha Spell
6. Anagrams
7. Analogies
8. Blueberries and Bananas
9. Body Words
10. Book It
11. Bright Ideas: Brainstorming
12. Change a Letter
13. Classifier
14. Commonalities
15. Compound It
16. Concentrate
17. Coordinating Concepts
18. Crazy Quizzes
19. Creative Problem Solving
20. Crosswords
21. Cube It
22. Daffynitions
23. Double Letters
24. Electroboards
25. Extemporaneously Speaking
26. Fact File
27. Find a Word in a Word
28. Fore and Aft
29. Graffiti Grammar Art
30. Graphic Organizers
31. Grouping Strategies
32. Hand Hopper Puzzle
33. Hide and Seek
34. Hink Pink
35. Homographs
36. Homophones
37. How Many Words From One
38. I Have; Who Has
39. Inside Outside Circles
40. Jeopardy
41. Jigsaw Juxtaposition
42. Jokes and Riddles
43. Journals
44. Ketchup and Mustard
45. Kinesthetic Name Game
46. KWL
47. Line Ups
48. Logic Puzzles
49. Mime and Model It
50. Mind Maps
51. Mini Unit
52. Mix Freeze Pair
53. Mnemonics
54. Mock Trial
55. Mysterious Messages
56. Name Game Alliterative Adjectives
57. Newspaper Reporter
58. No Vowels
59. Number Report
60. Oughtographs
61. Pair Interviews
62. Paired Problem Solving
63. Palindromes
64. People Searches
65. PMI Assessment
66. Rap It
67. S.C.A.M.P.E.R.
68. Six Hats
69. Songster
70. Sound Effects Story
71. Spellathon
72. Synonyms and Antonyms
73. $10,000 Pyramid
74. The Letter is a . .
75. 30 (or 50) Word Summary
76. Throw the Dice
77. Top Ten Lists
78. Toss the Ball
79. Triangle Listening Interviews
80. Turnabouts
81. 20 Questions
82. 26 Letters Missing
83. Venn Again
84. Warm Ups = WUPS
85. What Comes After?
86. What If . . ?
87. Word Pyramid
88. Word Scavenger Hunt
89. Write It
90. Wuzzles

Acknowledgements

I would like to express my appreciation to my children David and Courtney who not only listened to my "school" stories while seated at the dinner table for so many years, but who were also guinea pigs for many strategies and activities.

A special thanks to my wonderful husband Bruce who supports me in all my endeavors and makes sure my car is filled with gas before a workshop or presentation.

I would also like to thank my fabulous sister Linda, who is always encouraging and has undying faith in me.

Dedication

To my extraordinary mother Pinky Aaker 1922-2004
An inspiration to all . . . and a teacher.

How Do We Learn?

Recent research on the human brain is providing new understanding of how we learn.

Brain Facts

1. Your brain has about 100 billion active neurons.
2. Each neuron grows branches called dendrites.
3. One neuron can have up to 20,000 dendrites.
4. Each cell connects to other cells by sending electrical - chemical messages along axons.
5. The electrical impulses trigger the release of chemicals across a small gap call the synapse.
6. Each axon is covered with a myelin sheath, a fatty substance, which is like insulation around electrical wires. The better the sheathing or insulation, the faster the messages will speed along the wires.
7. The branching dendrites take in information and the axon carries it to other cells.
8. A neural network is made up of billions of neurons.
9. Neural networks are changed and grown and shaped by our experiences.

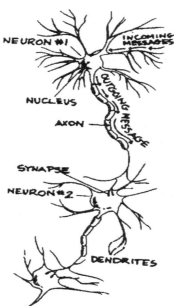

10. Each brain is unique.

Nerve cells, or neurons, enable our brain to make new connections and communicate with itself and with our entire body. We each have approximately 100 billion neurons in our brain. Each neuron is composed of a cell with a nucleus, a long fiber called an axon, and dendrites, which are shorter fibers that branch from the cell. These neurons form a network that is constantly growing and changing.

Neurons contain electrical impulses, somewhat like messages moving though telephone wires. The axons, which carry messages from the neurons, have a covering around them like insulation on electrical wire. The electrical impulses trigger the release of chemicals across a small gap call the synapse.

The chemical messengers are called neurotransmitters. The receptors on the receiving side of the synapse are shaped to receive certain neurotransmitters (chemicals) and to reject others.

Through practice, neurons grow in their ability to connect and communicate.

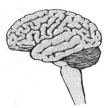

HOW WE LEARN

Memory, Learning and the Brain

The relationship between learning and memory are inextricably linked. According to Pat Wolfe (2001) the learning process involves four interrelated processes: sensory memory, limbic system, short-term memory, and long-term memory.

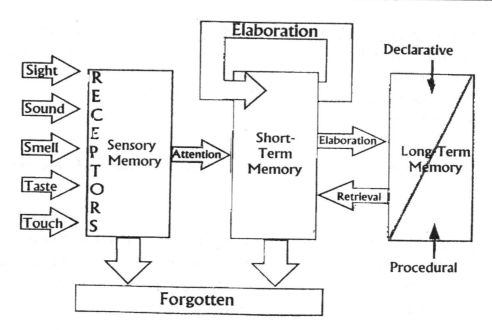

All information is brought in through our senses (sensory memory). The brain determines if the information is emotionally important (limbic system). If not, the information is dropped or forgotten. If the brain determines that the information is important, it stimulates brain cells which produce more neurotransmitters and strengthen synapses (short term memory). Neural networks are strengthened by repeated activation. This causes changes in the neural networks so that messages are sent more effectively and may become more permanent (long term memory).

Most sensory information is discarded immediately upon entering the brain. This is because the brain filters information that is irrelevant. Although the brain is sometimes referred to as a sponge that soaks up information, it is much more like a sieve. So how does the brain decide what to pay attention to and what to discard? One key factor in the filtering process is whether the incoming stimulus is different from what we are used to. Novelty, intensity (loud noises, a bright light) or movement will get the brain's attention for a short time. More important methods of getting and keeping attention are meaning or relevance and emotion.

According to Wolfe (2001) working memory is that portion of sensory memory that captures the brain's attention well enough that it allows you to become consciously aware of it. Working memory allows the learner to integrate the current information with stored knowledge and then manipulate this information so that it can be stored in long-term memory. In other words, the learner tries to make sense of the input, finding a pattern that enables the input to connect through neural pathways to other knowledge stored in the brain.

It is this manipulation of information that forms the basis of this book.

Rehearsal is any conscious manipulation of information: talking about it, thinking about it, writing about it, drawing or singing about it. Using a variety of strategies to rehearse information while making it relevant and meaningful to the learner will help build stronger neural pathways that have greater potential to be stored in long-term memory.

The brain compatible strategies in this book are based on brain research accompanied by the research and theory of the following thinking models.

Types of Thinking: Critical and Creative Thinking

Thinking skills have been grouped in many ways. For practical purposes they have been divided into two categories: critical and creative. Critical thinking is a convergent process that relies heavily on analysis and evaluation. It seeks to *narrow* ideas and options toward a single goal or solution. Creative thinking is a divergent process, which means to move outward or to *broaden* in many directions from a single point or even a single question.

Although critical and creative thinking have often been stereotyped as opposites, they are complementary ways of thinking. Solving problems involves both types of thinking – diverging and converging. Generating many ideas without analysis will not solve a problem; yet together, critical and creative thinking may lead to better solutions because of the choices and options that arise during the idea generation period.

Bloom's Taxonomy

Taxonomies can be defined as classification systems developed to delineate educational goals, objectives and outcomes. They provide a way to understand and develop questions. Because taxonomies are descriptions of types of behavior, they are observable in the classroom.

Bloom's six levels of thinking is a useful model from which to develop learning tasks. These range from a basic knowledge and understanding of a topic, to tasks that promote the development of higher order thinking skills such as evaluation. The six levels in his model are:
Knowledge, Comprehension, Application, Analysis, Synthesis, Evaluation

Knowledge
Recognize, list, describe, identify, retrieve, name...
Can the student **recall** information?

Comprehension
Interpret, exemplify, summarize, infer, paraphrase...
Can the student **explain** ideas or concepts?

Application
Implement, carry out, use...
Can the student **use** the new knowledge in another familiar situation?

Analysis
Compare, attribute, organize, deconstruct...
Can the student **differentiate** between constituent parts?

Synthesis
Design, construct, plan, produce...
Can the student **generate** new products, ideas or ways of viewing things?

Evaluation
Check, critique, judge, hypothesize...
Can the student **justify** a decision or course of action?

Williams' Taxonomy is another important model for teaching thinking skills and designing tasks. While Bloom's Taxonomy is used mostly for teaching critical thinking skills, William's Taxonomy is used for teaching creative thinking skills.

Although there is a relationship between these two models and even some overlap, it should be noted that critical thinking tends to be more reactive and vertical in nature while creative thinking tends to be more proactive and lateral in nature. Another way of saying this is that critical thinking tends to involve tasks that are logical, rational, sequential, and analytical and convergent. Creative thinking, on the other hand, involves tasks that are spatial, flexile, spontaneous, analogical, and divergent.

Williams' Taxonomy has eight levels also arranged in a hierarchy with certain types of student behavior associated with each level. The first four levels are cognitive in nature while the last four levels are affective in nature.

Cognitive Domain

Fluency	Generate oodles, scads, heaps, many ideas; how many?
Flexibility	Generate varied, different, alternative ideas: adapt, change, redirect
Originality	Generate unusual, clever, unique, novel, new ideas
Elaboration	Generate enriched, embellished, expanded ideas

Affective Domain

Risk Taking	Experiment with and explore ideas; take a chance, try new challenges
Complexity	Improve and explain ideas; create structure, order
Curiosity	Ponder and question ideas, wonder about options
Imagination	Visualize and fantasize possibilities and ideas

HOW TO USE THIS BOOK

The brain compatible strategies in this book are arranged in alphabetical order. Teachers may choose to write units of work, plugging in a strategy or strategies that work best with their theme or topic.

- Each page includes a short introduction.
- Next is a chart that identifies the brain links, brain processing preferences, content skills, and thinking skills.
- The **Brain Links** are based on the most recent research in cognitive and neuroscience.
- **Brain Processing Preferences** relate to Multiple Intelligences and learning style preferences present within the activity.
- The **Content Skill** column is the area that is directly related to tested skills on state assessments.
- The last column includes **Thinking Skills** that are required, introduced and/or reinforced when using the activity.

Brain Link	Brain Processing Preference	Content Skill	Thinking Skill

- Each activity lists the **materials** needed and **directions** to complete the activity followed by **examples**.

The Warm Up activities are designed for use each day at the start of the class period. This gives students an opportunity to begin thinking in the first two minutes of class and serves as a classroom management tool.

Strategies such as Creative Problem Solving, S.C.A.M.P.E.R. and Mini Units may be used as projects. Other strategies may take just fifteen minutes of class time. The activities and strategies address standards and are easily linked to a specific state's standards.

BRAIN LINKS

How the Brain Constructs Meaning
Our brain tries to make sense out of the world and is always seeking meaning from this outside information. Connecting information with other known information or with student interests or their personal life, adds relevance for the learner.

Activate Prior Knowledge
Learning needs to be linked to prior knowledge or experience for students to make sense of the information. Offer examples for students that relate to real world situations.

Attention and Focus
Attention and focus are the first steps to learning. Visuals, a story, music, novelty, humor, noisemakers, or props are first steps in getting and keeping student attention. During a lecture, have students talk about the information every 7-10 minutes, depending on their age.

Challenge and Problem Solving
The brain needs challenge and problem solving to grow new dendrites. All learning begins with a challenge.

Choice
When choice is offered, students have a sense of control over their learning and can reduce stress.

Engage Emotions
Emotions drive attention, meaning making, and play a role in memory formation. The stronger the emotion, the more meaning (of information) is likely to be constructed and stored in the brain.

Environment
The learning environment should be safe, physically and emotionally, with complete absence of threat. This is the first step to engaging positive emotion and attention from students. Providing consistent procedures, rituals and celebrations will help establish the best learning environment.

Feedback, Reflection and Evaluation

The brain survives on feedback. Give your students feedback every 30 minutes. Better still; provide ways for students to give each other feedback and design activities that allow for immediate feedback.

Humor

Laughter provides a state change and demands higher levels of thinking. Use cartoons, funny stories, picture books, props, or word play, such as puns, for novelty.

Mind Body Link

The brain was designed for the body to move. After 17 minutes of inactivity, the brain becomes sluggish and Melatonin is released throughout the body. This makes you sleepy! Movement will stop the Melatonin and increase focus and attentiveness.

Multiple Intelligences

Howard Gardner's theory of Multiple Intelligences provides a framework of how students learn and process information. When a variety of intelligences are included in instruction, students are more likely to remain engaged and retain the information. These intelligences include:

Verbal/Linguistic:	reading, writing, speaking, and listening
Mathematical/Logical:	working with numbers and patterns
Visual/Spatial:	working with images, mind maps, visualizing, and drawing
Musical/Rhythmic:	using rhythm melody, patterned sound, song, rap, dance
Bodily/Kinesthetic:	processing information through touch, movement, and dramatics
Interpersonal:	sharing, cooperating, interviewing, relating
Intrapersonal:	working alone, self-paced instruction, individualized projects
Naturalist:	spending time outdoors, sorting, classifying, noticing patterns

Multiple Memory Pathways

Information and experiences are stored in a variety of pathways. Consider using several strategies, such as visuals, movements or actions, partner discussions, or mind mapping when teaching important information. Utilize Gardner's Multiple Intelligences and learning style research.

Novelty

Novelty wakes up the brain and gets attention.

Pattern Seeking/Meaning Making

The brain is pattern seeking and is always trying to "hook" or "link" new information to previous or similar information or experiences.

Practice

Practice is necessary for the brain to make good connections so that it can store and retrieve information easily. For long term memory storage and retrieval, use a variety of learning style modalities.

Relevance

Relevance is how the student personally connects with the material. The brain learns best in real world learning situations and when the information has meaning for the learner. Connect to students' experiences and interests for engaging attention, emotion, and long lasting learning.

Sifting

In order for learning to stick, students need down time to consolidate and integrate learning. Sifting provides opportunities for students to share, discuss, draw, map, journal, teach or act out the learning. Allow for Sifting every 20 to 30 minutes during instruction. This will help students create personal meaning and a deeper understanding of the material.

Social Interaction

The brain is social. Use a range of gripping strategies. During lectures, educators should structure time for students to talk about the topic. An example would be, "Turn to your partner and tell them three reasons why..."

Variety

Provide multiple contexts for learning the same thing. The more ways we learn something the more likely the information will be stored and easily retrieved.

1. A TO Z LISTS

Intro: This is great activity to introduce a new unit and to find out what your students may already know about the topic. Students try to think of a word or phrase associated with the topic, matched to each letter of the alphabet. To use as a review, students list phrases and keywords related to the unit that they have studied.

Brain Link	Brain Processing Preference	Content Skill	Thinking Skill
Attention/Focus Practice Feedback Activate prior knowledge	Verbal/Linguistic Auditory Tactile Individual, small groups	Vocabulary Listening Research skills	Brainstorming Fluency Flexibility Risk taking

Materials: paper and pencil (Optional: dictionary, encyclopedias)

Activity: Have students list all the letters of the alphabet down a sheet of paper. Working individually, students write as many words or phrases associated with the topic. For instance, if the topic is animals, students might list A = anteater, B = bat, C = coyote, D = deer, E = emu, F = ferret, and so on. Give students adequate time to think, and then have them pair up or work in small groups to fill in the blanks.

Example: Media

A = antenna
B = BBC
C = channels
P = prime time
R = reception

This can be adapted to fit any age or ability group.

2. ACROSTIC FACTS

Intro: Even students who think they do not like poetry love acrostics! This is a short activity that forces students to think within a specified framework.

Brain Link	Brain Processing Preference	Content Skill	Thinking Skill
Practice Reflection	Verbal/Linguistic Analytic Individual	Vocabulary Research skills	Attributes Flexibility

Materials: paper and pencil (Optional: dictionary, encyclopedias, text books)

Activity: Students write facts using the first letters of a theme or topic related word.

Example: Theme: Countries

A	Aborigine
U	Uluru
S	Sharks
T	Tasmanian Devil
R	Rainforests and Reef
A	Adelaide
L	Lyrebird
I	Island
A	Ayers Rock

Variation: Students write questions for further research about the topic.

3. ADD A LETTER

Intro: This activity will keep your students engaged while reinforcing spelling or vocabulary skills.

Brain Link	Brain Processing Preference	Content Skill	Thinking Skill
Novelty Challenge Practice Pattern seeking	Verbal/Linguistic Analytic Individual	Word study Vocabulary Listening Spelling Rhyming	Analysis

Materials: paper and pencil

Activity: Students add a letter to the given word to make a new word. Content-related vocabulary or spelling words may be used as either the base word or the new word formed.

Examples:

Add an A and rearrange the letters to get a word that fits the definitions.

Add an A to LET and get a story (tale)

Add an A to BEST to get an animal (beast)

Add a G and rearrange the letters to get a word that fits the definitions.

Add a G to POUR and get a number of people together (group)

Add a G to BAR and get boast (brag)

Add a C and rearrange the letters to get a word that fits the definitions.

Add a C to TREES and get what you can't tell anyone (secret)

Add a C and rearrange the letters to get a word that fits the definitions.

Add a C to TANS and get not enough (scant)

Add a Y to REAL and a kind of race (relay)

Add a Y to TOAD and get right now (today)

Variation: Rhyming Add A Letter

A London mist is called a _____ (fog)

Add a letter for a croaking green _____ (frog)

You use a key to open a _____ (lock)

Add a letter to tell time on a _____ (clock)

One-twelfth of a foot is called an _____ (inch)

Add a letter for a small squeeze or _____ (pinch)

4. ADD A WORD

Intro: Students will need to read and think critically to solve these word puzzles.

Brain Link	Brain Processing Preference	Content Skill	Thinking Skill
Challenge Practice Pattern seeking Activate prior knowledge	Verbal/Linguistic Analytic Individual	Word study Vocabulary Spelling Synonyms Rhyming Critical reading	Analysis

Materials: paper and pencil

Activity: Students add a complete word between the given letters to make a new word that fits the definition.

Examples:
Add *ADORE* to get what you wear on your hands

    G ___ ___ ___ ___ S   (love to gloves)

Add *play the part of* to get truthful information

    F ___ ___ ___ S   (act to facts)

Add *jumps on one foot* to get places in a mall

    S ___ ___ ___ S   (hop to shops)

Add *the opposite of OUT* and get what belongs to me   (in to mine)

    M ___ ___ E

5. ALPHA SPELL

Intro: Students love puzzles. This activity will make learning spelling and vocabulary words fun.

Brain Link	Brain Processing Preference	Content Skill	Thinking Skill
Challenge Practice Pattern seeking Activate prior knowledge	Verbal/Linguistic Analytic Individual	Word study Vocabulary Spelling	Analysis

Materials: paper and pencil

Activity: Create vocabulary or spelling lists where the letters in the words are in alphabetical order. Students unscramble the letters to find the word.

Variation: Classify words into four categories and give the categories titles.

Examples:
ABIGHOPY = BIOGRAPHY
NNOU = NOUN

6. ANAGRAMS OR REARRANGING WORDS

Intro: An anagram is a word or phrase made by transposing or rearranging the letters of a word or phrase to create another.

Brain Link	Brain Processing Preference	Content Skill	Thinking Skill
Challenge Practice Pattern seeking Activate prior knowledge	Verbal/Linguistic Analytic Individual	Word study Vocabulary Spelling	Analysis

Materials: paper and pencil

Activity: In this activity students rearrange letters of words or phrases to form new ones.

Example:

own	now
decal	laces
shot	host
devil	lived
coast	tacos
cheat	teach
fear	fare
spear	reaps, pears, spare
smile	miles, limes, slime
listen	tinsel, enlist, inlets, silent
eats	east, seat, teas
scare	races, acres, cares
a small bet	meatballs
dirty room	dormitory
Alas! No more Zs	snooze alarms

Topic: Careers

stripe	priest
cheater	teacher
try a note	attorney
our hat	author
pertain	painter
scary tree	secretary

7. ANALOGIES

Intro: Analogies require students to see relationships between words and concepts. These relationships may span from the very simple to the very complex, often requiring the student to formulate precise relationships between two word groups that are very different.

Brain Link	Brain Processing Preference	Content Skill	Thinking Skill
Challenge Practice Pattern seeking	Verbal/Linguistic Analytical Individual	Word study Vocabulary Opposites Analogies Comprehension	Problem solving Analysis Cause/Effect Compare/Contrast Fact/Opinion

In order to solve analogy puzzles, students must consider how the first two items relate to each other and then complete the second set of words by finding a word that relates in the same way.
Say: "____ is related to ____ in the same way that ____ is related to ____."
Fact is related to real in the same way that fiction is related to pretend.

The most common analogies are:
1. Parts of a whole: thumb is to hand as big toe is to foot
2. Opposites: high is to low as up is to down
3. What it does: sing is to voice as dance is to legs
4. Category or type: Labrador is to dog as Persian is to cat
5. Almost the same: plan is to route as plot is to course
6. What it is used for: knife is to cut as hammer is to pound
7. Difference in degree: warm is to hot as cool is to cold

Materials: paper and pencil

Activity: Have students write analogies using vocabulary terms, spelling words, grammar rules, punctuation marks, elements in a novel, characters, or for a content concept. Allow students to exchange papers to solve classmates' analogies.

8. BLUEBERRIES AND BANANAS

Intro: This activity makes deciphering context clues and writing sentences fun! Students will try to stump their classmates.

Brain Link	Brain Processing Preference	Content Skill	Thinking Skill
Challenge Practice Humor Feedback	Verbal/Linguistic Analytic Individual, pairs, small groups	Word study Vocabulary Spelling Writing Reading Context clues	Comprehension Flexibility Prediction

Materials: spelling or vocabulary lists, paper and pencil

Activity: Use your spelling words or vocabulary words to make blueberry and banana sentences. Write a spelling or vocabulary word in a sentence and then substitute the word 'blueberry' or 'banana' for the actual word. Give your sentences to a classmate to see if he or she can figure out the real words.

Variations:
Make it more difficult by using more than one spelling word in a sentence. Using your vocabulary or spelling words, make as few sentences as possible using all of the words on the list.

9. BODY WORDS

Intro: This lively activity will get kids up and moving. It is a motivating way to introduce a new concept or unit.

Brain Link	Brain Processing Preference	Content Skill	Thinking Skill
Novelty Challenge Practice Social interaction Pattern seeking	Verbal/Linguistic Bodily/Kinesthetic Analytic Small Groups	Word study Vocabulary	Problem solving Originality Analysis Risk taking

Materials: paper and pencil, spelling or content related words

Activity: Students are divided into groups and each member is given a piece of paper with a large letter written on it. Students must form words by rearranging themselves in the correct letter order of the new word. Discuss the meaning of the concept and introduce the topic to be studied. This is also a good time to review cooperation within groups.

P	O	W	E	R	S

Variation: Students find as many words as they can from a letter grid and points are awarded on length of words.

F	I	N	E	I
J	T	I	E	O
D	E	S	E	L
W	L	T	F	I
I	D	U	E	N

10. BOOK IT!

Intro: Give students choice and variety in the way they present their book or research reports. This hands-on activity encourages your students to think differently whether writing a report or an original story.

Brain Link	Brain Processing Preference	Content Skill	Thinking Skill
Challenge Choice/Variety Novelty	Verbal/Linguistic Visual/Spatial Tactile Artistic Individual	Comprehension Writing Summarizing Paraphrasing Punctuation Grammar	Analyzing Synthesizing Evaluating Designing Organizing

Materials: construction paper, scissors, glue, tape, hole punch, yarn, or string

Activity: Students write, illustrate and share their original books or research reports and/or original stories in this activity.

Shape books: Trace and cut a shape onto writing paper and two pieces of construction paper for covers. Staple pages or use a hole punch and tie together. Shape Ideas: animals, house, flip flops, mittens, t-shirt, cloud, bus, spaceship, etc.

Three part fold out books: Cut writing paper to fit the center section. Cut one piece of construction paper the same shape and cut down the center for opening. Example: Castle or an Open House

Accordion Books: Begin with a strip of 6 X 18 construction paper folded into quarters. Tape 4 1/2 X 5 pieces of tag board to the front and back to create a cover. Cover ends can be cut in any shape. Glue writing paper to each accordion square.

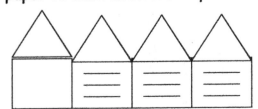

Flap books:

Answer under flap
Why did the chicken cross the playground?

11. BRIGHT IDEAS: BRAINSTORMING

Intro: Brainstorming is a technique that allows for students to generate ideas, answers, or solutions to problems.

Brain Link	Brain Processing Preference	Content Skill	Thinking Skill
Attention/Focus Meaning making Relevance Trigger emotions	Verbal/Linguistic Analytic Individual, small groups	All	Brainstorming Fluency Flexibility Elaboration Risk taking Analysis

Materials: paper and pencil

Activity: Teacher chooses a topic to brainstorm. Be creative!

Examples: In ten minutes, brainstorm ways to show thanks. Count your fluency and flexibility points.

Brainstorm at least 10 uses for an old turkey carcass and draw a picture using your most original idea.

Brainstorm new ideas and uses for a zipper.

Brainstorm things that begin with the letter B.

Brainstorm words that start with the letter S and end with the letter E.

Brainstorm words that start with the letter L and end with the letter T.

Brainstorm words that begin with the letter M and end with the letter N.

Brainstorm occupations that require hats.

Brainstorm 10 negative things you often say about other people or situations. Reword them into positive statements.

How many different types of hats can you name in 2 minutes?

Brainstorm uses for an empty can; a pencil; a spoon; a hanger, a toilet paper roll.

Brainstorm what a thingamajig could be.

What do you do with an old Christmas tree? Brainstorm 10 possibilities and illustrate your most original.

Thinking is like _____ because.... Write at least five (5) similes for "thinking."

A problem is like _____ because.... Write at least 5 similes.

Write four (4) similes and one (1) analogy for Spring Break.

Write an analogy for each of the following words: invent, inventor, invention.

Create three (3) similes for each statement: Facing problems is like...

Brainstorming alternatives is like... Finding solutions is like....

Brainstorm sets of homonyms.

Brainstorm things that bounce.

Brainstorm things made from a potato.

Brainstorm things that are soft and yellow.

Brainstorm things that have a button to push.

Brainstorm words that have double consonants.

12. CHANGE A LETTER

<u>Intro</u>: One letter makes a difference! Beginning sounds, vowel and consonant sounds, and spelling skills are reinforced in this activity.

Brain Link	Brain Processing Preference	Content Skill	Thinking Skill
Attention/Focus Meaning making	Verbal/Linguistic Analytic Individual	All	Fluency Analysis

<u>Materials</u>: paper and pencil

<u>Activity</u>: Change one letter of the word to make a new word.

<u>Examples</u>:

	Answers			Answers
BOAT	GOAT		HALF	CALF
SONG	SING		SHAKE	SHAME
DIME	LIME		AXE	APE
LOST	LAST		WHOLE	WHILE
CRUST	CREST		DISH	WISH, FISH

13. CLASSIFIER

Intro: This activity forces students to think critically about commonalities and differences.

Brain Link	Brain Processing Preference	Content Skill	Thinking Skill
Pattern seeking Meaning making Relevance Practice	Verbal/Linguistic Analytic Individual	All	Analysis Flexibility Elaboration Categorizing

Materials: paper and pencil

Activity: Students provide as many ways of categorizing aspects of a theme and then draw a chart, matrix, or diagram giving examples in each.

Example: Occupations
Put the following occupations into categories. What is the common attribute for each category?

Carpet layer	Truck driver	dentist	airline pilot
Accountant	Photographer	banker	gardener
Cook	nurse	teacher	artist
TV newscaster	salesperson	architect	mayor

14. COMMONALITIES

Intro: In this activity students will be surprised at what they have in common with each other.

Brain Link	Brain Processing Preference	Content Skill	Thinking Skill
Pattern seeking Meaning making Practice	Verbal/Linguistic Analytic Whole class	All	Observe Analysis Attributes Categorizing

Materials: none

Activity: Ask students wearing glasses, with curly hair, or the same height to stand together and have the class guess what they have in common.

Variation: Students are required to identify common characteristics of a group of words and then name the common group to which they belong. What characteristics do the words on each line have in common?

Theme: Language Arts   **Answers**

princess, giant, witch, castle   _____   fairy tales
and, but, nor, or   _____   conjunctions
of, about, into, under   _____   prepositions
noun, verb, adjective, adverb   _____   parts of speech
beginning, middle, end   _____   story, essay, movie
period, comma, colon, parentheses _____   punctuation
sonnet, limerick, haiku   _____   forms of poetry

15. COMPOUND IT

Intro: Get students thinking at a higher level about compound words. Make the activity a mystery by giving clues.

Brain Link	Brain Processing Preference	Content Skill	Thinking Skill
Challenge Novelty Practice Activate prior knowledge Pattern seeking	Verbal/Linguistic Visual Tactile Individual	Word study Compounds Vocabulary Spelling Contextual clues	Problem solving Analysis

Materials: paper and pencil

Activity: Students form compound words using given letters. The words may begin in either direction. Use compound words from a novel and write clues that offer story details.

Example: The following are from <u>Harry Potter and the Philosopher's Stone</u>.

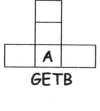
GETB

Clue: Hagrid carried one of these in his coat pocket.

Answer: Teabag

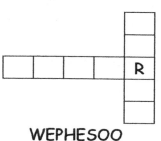
WEPHESOO

Clue: The Nimbus 2000 has more of this than the Comet Two Sixty.

Answer: Horsepower

Variation: Mystery Compound Words

Try to solve the mystery compound word based on the clue that is given in two parts. Have students write mystery clues for classmates to solve.

Part 1: not tall, but ____   Part 2: to slice or break ____   (shortcut)

Part 1: opposite of hard ____ Part 2: round object ____   (softball)

Part 1: wide ____   Part 2: actors in a play ____   (broadcast)

16. CONCENTRATE, CONTEMPLATE & RECALL

Intro: Hands-on learning with a partner! The brain learns best when it experiences the information in a variety of ways. This activity offers practice and allows for appropriate social interaction. Bring in appropriate competition using your content vocabulary, concepts or spelling words.

Brain Link	Brain Processing Preference	Content Skill	Thinking Skill
Challenge Practice Social interaction Pattern seeking	Verbal/Linguistic Visual Tactile Pairs	Word study Vocabulary Cause/Effect Fact/Opinion Letter recognition	Recall/remembering Comprehension

Materials: Prepare cards in pairs with matching information
Pictures, words, letters or numbers can be used.

Activity: Concentration requires an even number of players. Prepare cards in pairs with matching information and lay face down on table. Student looks at one card and tries to find its match. If a match is not made, the card is returned, facedown, to the same spot on the board. When a match is made, that player keeps the pair. The player with the most pairs wins.

Examples:

Letters: One card with a letter and another with a picture of a word that starts with that letter. (R   raincoat)

Time: One card with a clock face showing the time and another with numbers

Fractions: One card with the fraction (1/3) number and another card with a circle shaded to show that fraction.

More options: Synonyms, homonyms, foreign language words, vocabulary and definitions

17. COORDINATING CONCEPTS

Intro: Each individual brain needs to make its own meaning. This vocabulary activity makes learning relevant for students.

Brain Link	Brain Processing Preference	Content Skill	Thinking Skill
Relevance Practice Pattern seeking Multiple memory pathways	Verbal/Linguistic Visual Tactile Individual, pair, small groups	Vocabulary Opposites Analogies Comprehension	Problem solving Analysis Cause/Effect Compare/Contrast Fact/Opinion

Materials: paper, scissors, dictionary, thesaurus or textbook, magazines, markers or crayons

Activity: Task cards are two- or three-part puzzles that are related. **Examples:** cause and effect, picture and word, definition and word, etc. Give students a list of words that need to be defined and a heavy strip of paper divided into three parts. Ask students to write one of the words in the left box, and then write a definition or synonyms in the middle box. Find a picture or draw an illustration of that word in the last box.

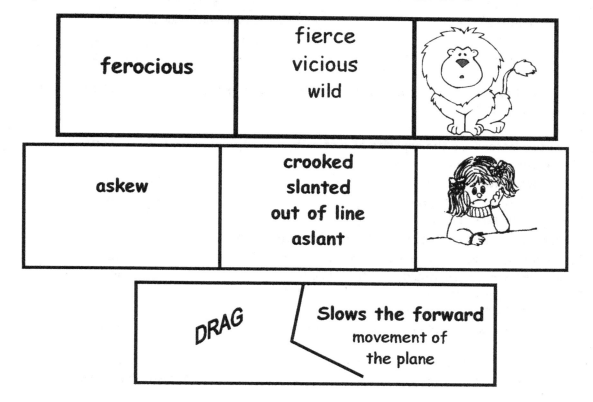

18. CRAZY QUIZZES

Intro: Surprise students with a crazy quiz that will keep them thinking and engage their curiosity.

Brain Link	Brain Processing Preference	Content Skill	Thinking Skill
Pattern seeking Meaning making Challenge	Mathematical/Logical Verbal/Linguistic Analytic Individual, pairs	Vocabulary Spelling	Problem solving Analysis

Activity: Design crazy quizzes using the following examples.

Instructions: Each question below contains the initials of words that will make it correct. Find the missing words. For example: 12 M in a Y would be 12 months in a year.

1.	26 = L of the A	1.	26 letters of the alphabet
2.	7 = Y of B L for B a M	2.	7 years bad luck for breaking a mirror
3.	1001 = A N	3.	1,001 Arabian Nights
4.	54 = C in a D (with J's)	4.	54 cards in a deck with jokers
5.	88 = P K	5.	88 piano keys
6.	200= D for P G in M	6.	200 dollars for passing go in Monopoly
7.	8 = S on a S S	7.	8 sides on a stop sign
8.	9 = P in the S S	8.	9 planets in the Solar System
9.	3 = B M (S H T R)	9.	3 blind mice; see how they run
10.	7 = W of the A W	10.	7 Wonders of the Ancient World

This quiz makes words out of letter sounds. Write the letter or letters and the word next to each definition.

Answers

1. These two letters are the opposite of difficult	E Z	easy
2. This letter is a large body of water	C	sea
3. These two letters can make a tooth ache.	D K	decay
4. These two letters mean jealousy.	N V	envy
5. These two letters are what is no longer full.	M T	empty

Unscramble the letters to answer the questions

1. If you pitched a NETT, would a catcher be handy to have?	tent
2. If an ADEI struck you, would you strike back?	idea
3. If you gave your mother a LAUH PHOO, would she cook it?	Hula hoop
4. If your THWAC spread out its hands and ran, would you chase it?	watch
5. If someone tossed a DASAL, would you catch it?	salad

Using every letter in the word **ASTRONOMERS** just once, can you make three words that would make astronomers sad?   Answer: **No more stars**

19. CREATIVE PROBLEM SOLVING

Intro: Creative Problem Solving is a thinking model that guides students in solving problems in an effective and imaginative way.

Brain Link	Brain Processing Preference	Content Skill	Thinking Skill
Challenge Choice/Variety Trigger emotions Relevance Social interaction	Verbal/Linguistic Mathematical/Logical Global Analytic Groups	All	Problem solving Sequence Analysis Synthesis Evaluation Originality Composing

Materials: CPS outline below

Activity: Using a theme or relevant curriculum topic, pose a conflict issue, question, or problem. Below are possible issues to use with the CPS model.

♦ How can school crossings be improved so that they are safer for children to cross?

♦ Approximately one-quarter of the world's population is starving or seriously malnourished. What can be done to rectify this situation?

♦ You and your best friend are shopping. As you turn around you see your friend take something without paying for it. You tell your friend that you saw what she did, but your friend says it's all right because she didn't get caught. You know it is not right.

♦ The sun has been shining for twenty-four hours a day on planet Earth. Experts predict that this is to remain permanent.

The CPS Model

1. Fact Finding:

   Who? What? Where? When? Why? How? Consider resources that may help students find answers to questions.

2. Problem Finding:

   The aim is to clarify and define the major problem. Students may speculate on possible problems from several viewpoints, decide on the most critical problem, and restate the problem that accurately defines it. It should be worded as, "In what ways might we . . ."

- What is the problem?
- Define all the problems about the scenario.
- Decide which is the most important problem.
- Restate the problem.

3. Idea Finding:

Brainstorm as many ideas, strategies, alternatives, ways, and solutions as you can for this problem.

Remember that when you brainstorm:

(a) ALL ideas should be written down,

(b) No answers are wrong, and

(c) You should not make decisions about your responses at this point.

4. Solution Finding:

As a group, decide on criteria for judging your ideas.

Apply the criteria you have chosen to your solution. (Criteria will vary according to the problem.)

5. Acceptance Finding:

Solutions are ranked from best to worst for each criteria (1 = best). When finished, add across the grid for each solution to find its final ranking (low score is best).

SOLUTIONS	CRITERIA FOR SELECTION				TOTALS
	cost	time	works	looks	

Next:

- Develop a plan of action.
- Evaluate any problems that may be encountered.
- Evaluate all the concerns of people involved in your solution.

20. CROSSWORDS

Intro: Learning required vocabulary definitions using crossword puzzles engages students at a higher level of thinking.

Brain Link	Brain Processing Preference	Content Skill	Thinking Skill
Challenge Practice	Verbal/Linguistic Visual/Spatial Tactile Individual, pairs	Reading Organizing Following directions	Problem solving Sequence Analysis Composing

Materials: paper and pencil

Activity: Give students a list of words related to a theme or a topic. Students write clues for the word list. Using graph paper, students draw and number the squares to fit the connecting words into the puzzle.

Variation: Give students a completed crossword puzzle using words from a unit topic. Students write the clues only.

21. CUBE IT

Intro: CUBE IT encourages students to think about a given subject from six specifically identified perspectives.

Brain Link	Brain Processing Preference	Content Skill	Thinking Skill
Challenge Choice/Variety Trigger emotions Relevance	Verbal/Linguistic Visual/Spatial Tactile Artistic Individual	Reading Organizing Writing Summarizing Following directions	Problem solving Sequence Analysis Synthesis Evaluation Originality Composing

Materials: Pattern in index

Activity: Using a cube pattern, students write responses to theme related questions. For example, when studying a novel the cube might ask story element questions or if studying historical events the cube might ask Who? What? Where? When? How? Why? questions.

Variations: Use the cube sections to:
♦ Write a set of directions.
♦ Reflect on personal feelings, opinions, thoughts or aspects of a topic.
♦ Sequence story events through drawings.

Example:
Describe
Compare/ Contrast
Analyze
Associate
Apply
Argue

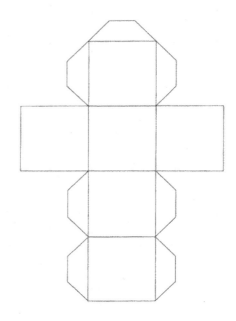

22. DAFFYNITIONS

Intro: Motivate your students with Daffynitions. Creating humorous definitions for spelling or vocabulary words will keep the class in stitches.

Brain Link	Brain Processing Preference	Content Skill	Thinking Skill
Challenge Choice/Variety Trigger emotions Relevance Humor	Verbal/Linguistic Individual, pairs	All	Problem solving Analysis Synthesis Originality Risk taking

Materials: paper and pencil

Activity: Use vocabulary or spelling word lists, or unit themes and topics, for students to create unusual and humorous definitions.

Examples:

Cannibal: something that can be put or stored in cans
Caterpillar: a worm wearing a sweater
Mischief: the Chief's daughter
Intense: a place where campers sleep
Baloney: where some dresses fall
Subdued: a cool guy who works on a submarine
Relief: what trees do in the spring
Carpet: any animal that likes to ride in a car
Bulldozer: sleeping steer
Housecoat: wrap for your dwelling
Carsick: car that needs a doctor

Theme: Law

Burglarize: what a crook sees with
Control: a short, ugly inmate
Counterfeiters: workers who put together kitchen cabinets
Sudafed: brought litigation against a government official
Appeal: outer area of an apple
Arbitrator: a cook that leaves Arby's® to work at Wendy's®
Kidnap: **small child's sleep**

23. DOUBLE LETTERS

Intro: This activity will keep your students engaged while reinforcing spelling rules.

Brain Link	Brain Processing Preference	Content Skill	Thinking Skill
Novelty Challenge Practice Pattern seeking	Verbal/Linguistic Analytic Individual	Word study Vocabulary Listening Spelling	Analysis

Materials: paper and pencil

Activity: Students fill in the words that fit the clues. Use vocabulary or spelling words.

		Answers
What you do if you have a cold	__ __ EE __ __	sneeze
A puzzle with words	__ __ DD __ __	riddle
A turkey's talk	__ __ BB __ __	gobble
An orange vegetable	__ __ RR __ __	carrot
Ordinary	__ __ MM __ __	common
Old fashioned hat	__ __ NN __ __	bonnet

Theme: Health Topic: Sports

A runner	__ __ GG __ __	jogger
A snow sport	__ __ II __ __	skiing
European football	__ __ CC __ __	soccer
What a bicycle must have	__ __ EE __ __	wheels
Touchdown game	__ OO __ __ __ LL	football
Golfers equipment	__ __ TT __ __	putter

24. ELECTROBOARDS

Intro: The brain needs immediate feedback while learning. Electroboards provide immediate visual feedback with a globe that lights up whenever the chosen answer is correct. Students love to make Electroboards and exchange them with fellow classmates. Electroboards make drill and practice fun.

Brain Link	Brain Processing Preference	Content Skill	Thinking Skill
Relevance Practice Multiple memory pathways Feedback	Tactile/ Kinesthetic Visual Individual, pair, small groups	Reading Language development Word study Vocabulary	Problem solving Following directions Organizing Analysis Cause/Effect Compare/Contrast Fact/Opinion

Materials: hole punch, heavy paper or tag board, scissors, masking tape, aluminum foil

Procedure

1. Cut two pieces of poster board into identical shapes.
2. Write the questions on the left-hand side of one piece of the poster board. Be sure to leave approximately four centimeters blank on the edge of the left-hand side.
3. Write or paste the answers in random order on the right-hand side of the same piece of poster board. Be sure to leave space on the right-hand edge.
4. Punch holes nearest the <u>outside</u> edge of each answer and question in both columns.
5. On the back, connect each beginning phrase or question with its proper ending or answer using a strip of aluminum foil or fuse wire. Cover each strip completely with masking tape before doing the next strip.
6. Using a continuity tester, check each circuit before connecting the next.
7. Once each question has been linked to each answer and has been tested, paste the second piece of poster board on the back to cover all masking tape or connections.

Example: Fairy Tales

O	Many folktales contain a _____ which is solved by clever behavior.	heroine	O
O	The ability of animals to speak and act in the same way humans do is called _____.	threes	O
O	A character admired for his actions is the _____.	hero	O
O	Folktales often end _____.	happily	O
O	Two characteristics of folktales are:	personification	O
O	The lady who is admired for the wonderful things she does is a _____.	typical opening line	O
O	"A long time ago" is an example of a _____.	riddle	O
O	_____ are an important part of the literature and culture for all groups of people.	good vs. evil	O
O	In folktales, events often occur in _____.	folktales	O
O	Many folktales have a common theme that deals with _____.	animals with human traits and heroes	O

25. EXTEMPORANEOUSLY SPEAKING

Intro: This is a fast and fun activity that helps students organize and express their feelings and ideas about a variety of topics.

Brain Link	Brain Processing Preference	Content Skill	Thinking Skill
Novelty Challenge Pattern seeking Humor	Verbal/Linguistic Analytic

Whole class | Speaking Listening | Elaboration Finding patterns Originality Risk taking |

Materials: none

Activity: Who knows what a cauldron is? Could you describe what a cauldron looks like? What does it feel like? How is it made? How do you use a cauldron? What are your experiences using a cauldron? How long do you think you could talk about cauldrons? Could you talk for a whole minute? You will have 10 seconds to think about a topic that is suggested by a classmate, then one minute to talk. We will time you using the second hand on the wall clock. If you stop talking for more than three seconds, your time will be up. The record keeper will keep track of how long you were able to speak extemporaneously!

Students may suggest any topic from chairs to zucchini.

Remind students that good speakers should stand tall, look at their audience, and speak loudly enough to be heard by the group. A good audience is quiet and looks at the speaker.

26. FACT FILE

Intro: Make research simple. In this activity, students create a fact file about a theme that can be used for many other activities or assignments.

Brain Link	Brain Processing Preference	Content Skill	Thinking Skill
Practice	Verbal/Linguistic Analytic Individual	Word study Research skills	Analysis Organizing skills

Materials: paper, pencil, and note cards

Activity: Students use note cards to make a facts file. This information can be used for reviewing material, partner teaching, trivia questions, concept puzzles, crosswords, report writing, etc.

27. FIND A WORD IN A WORD: HIDDEN SYNONYMS

Intro: This activity is a novel way for students to review vocabulary words and use higher level thinking skills.

Brain Link	Brain Processing Preference	Content Skill	Thinking Skill
Novelty Challenge Pattern seeking	Verbal/Linguistic Analytic Individual	Word study Vocabulary Spelling	Analysis

Materials: paper and pencil

Activity: In this activity synonyms are camouflaged or hidden within another word. The smaller word will be found in the correct spelling order, but not necessarily next to each other.

Examples: **Answers**

exist   is
blossom   bloom
totally   all
container   can

Theme: Mental Health Topic: Emotions, Motivation, Behavior

encourage   urge
joviality   joy
fallacies   lies
respite   rest
rampage   rage
salvage   save
observe   see
posture   pose
curtail   cut
regulate   rule

28. FORE AND AFT

Intro: Students stay engaged in this activity that looks like a game yet reinforces spelling and vocabulary skills.

Brain Link	Brain Processing Preference	Content Skill	Thinking Skill
Novelty Challenge Pattern seeking	Verbal/Linguistic Analytic Individual	Word study Vocabulary Spelling	Analysis

Materials: paper and pencil

Activity: Students fill in the missing letters to complete the words that fit the definitions. In each word the first and last letters are the same.

		Answers
A fragrance	A __ __ __ A	aroma
The back part	R __ __ R	rear
Lawful	L __ __ __ L	legal
Foot strike	K __ __ __ K	kick
Copy machine trade name	X __ __ __ X	Xerox
Well-rounded	P __ __ __ P	plump
Fit to eat	E __ __ __ __ E	edible
Stems of plants	S __ __ __ __ S	stalks
Small quarrels	S __ __ __ S	spats

Variation:

What you wear on your feet	__ hoe__	shoes
Outshine	__clips _	eclipse
Happy faces	__ mile__	smiles

Variation: First and last letters are not the same letter.

A splinter	__ live __	sliver
Manufacturing plant	__ actor__	factory
Move along smoothly	__lid__	glide
Thrust into water	__ lung __	plunge

29. GRAFFITI GRAMMAR ART

Intro: In this activity, students practice their knowledge of adjectives, nouns, verbs, and adverbs. They write the words artistically to provide a visual representation.

Brain Link	Brain Processing Preference	Content Skill	Thinking Skill
Novelty Multiple memory pathways	Visual/Spatial Artistic Tactile Individual	Grammar	Comprehension Imagination Creating

Materials: crayons or markers and paper

Activity: Students think of an adjective, noun, verb, or adverb based on the part of speech being studied. They then write the word in a way that represents the meaning of the word. They should use colors to further enhance the activity.

30. GRAPHIC ORGANIZERS

Intro: Graphic organizers help students organize their thoughts and information about specific topics. Tables, flow charts, webs, pro/con, and Venn diagrams are the most common organizers.

Brain Link	Brain Processing Preference	Content Skill	Thinking Skill
Attention/focus Activate prior knowledge Pattern seeking Multiple memory pathways Relevance	Verbal/Linguistic Visual Tactile Individual, pairs or small groups	Reading Language development Writing	Organizing skills Brainstorming Attributes Integrating skills

Materials: paper, markers or colored pencils

Activity: Have students analyze or sequence a story, character or concept using a graphic organizer.

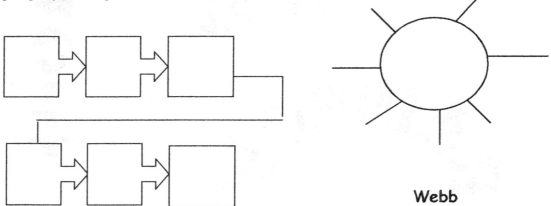

Flow Chart

Webb

31. GROUPING STRATEGIES OR THE MORE THE MERRIER!

Intro: This is a great activity to get students learning, reviewing, and moving while getting into groups.

Brain Link	Brain Processing Preference	Content Skill	Thinking Skill
Activate prior knowledge Social interaction	Bodily/Kinesthetic Class or large group	All	Problem solving Attributes Classify

Materials: Deck of cards, pictures cut into pieces, note cards, familiar songs, forms of words (agree, agreeable, agreement, agreed), Countries (France, Eiffel Tower, Seine River, Paris)

Theme related groups: The main idea or central theme of 3 or 4 words is written on a card and placed on a table. As students enter the room, hand them a card with a word that relates to one of the themes. A group is formed when the students go to the table that matches their words.

Forces of Flight	Lift	Drag
	Gravity	Thrust

A group of 4 is formed.

FRANCE	Eiffel Tower	Seine River	Paris

A group of 3 is formed.

Deck of Cards

Use a deck of cards to group students. Then ask all the Kings, Aces, Jacks etc. to form a group of four. Assign roles.

♠   Captain   Leader/Spokesperson
♦   Flight Attendant   Encourager/Praiser
♣   First Officer   Checker/Task Master
♣   Maintenance Engineer   Recorder (Black Box)

Theme: Flight

Smith, J.A. (2002). *Flying in style with attitude, aptitude and altitude*. Melbourne, VIC:

32. HAND HOPPER PUZZLE

Intro: Following directions and reviewing material is great fun using the hand hopper!

Brain Link	Brain Processing Preference	Content Skill	Thinking Skill
Novelty Challenge Social interaction	Visual /Spatial Artistic Tactile Individual, pairs	All	Following directions Analysis Originality Organization

Materials: Paper, scissors, crayons or markers

Activity: Students follow detailed instructions to make a paper model of the Hand Hopper puzzle. Select a topic and have students draw a symbol on the outside of each of the four outside flaps. Write the numbers 1 to 8 on each of the inside flaps. Lift the flap and write the answer to that question underneath the flap.

1. Use a large square piece of paper.
2. Find the middle of paper by folding it into 4 triangles and then unfold.
3. Fold each corner to the center point.
4. Flip over the piece of paper to the other side and repeat step 3.
5. Flip the paper over again and fold it into four squares, unfold it once so you have a rectangle.
6. Put a finger under each square flap and push the top corner into the middle.
7. Put a different symbol related to your topic on each of the four outside flaps.
8. Write the number 1 to 8 on the 8 inside flaps and write a question on your topic for each number.
9. Lift up the flap and write the answer underneath. Use a separate question and answer sheet if there is not enough room.

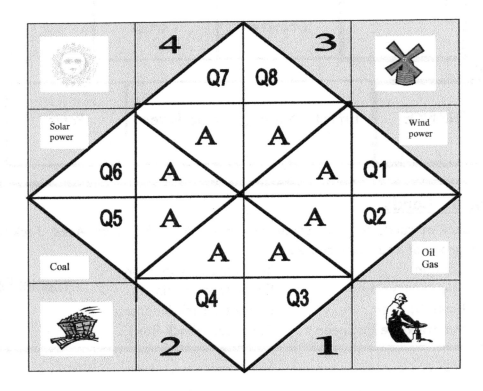

© Pieces of Learning

33. HIDE AND SEEK

<u>Intro</u>: Critical reading is fun and challenging with this activity.

Brain Link	Brain Processing Preference	Content Skill	Thinking Skill
Novelty Challenge Pattern Seeking	Verbal/Linguistic Analytic Individual	Reading Vocabulary	Analysis

<u>Materials</u>: pencil and paper

<u>Activity</u>: A name of a food, animal, explorer, or part of speech is hidden in each sentence, either in the middle of one word or by combining the end of one word with the beginning of the next.

<u>Examples</u>:

Insects

The performance <u>was</u> <u>p</u>erfect.   (wasp)
The hunter set the tr<u>ap, hid</u> in the bushes, and waited quietly.   (aphid)
While sitting too close to the camp<u>fire, fly</u>ing sparks burnt my   (firefly)
jacket.

Careers:

I enjoy Madonna's music, <u>but Cher</u> sings better.   (butcher)
You must coun<u>t each er</u>ror when you grade the quiz.   (teacher)
A story may be f<u>act or</u> fiction.   (actor)

Ocean Fish

Jessica wanted to <u>stun all</u> her friends at the party with her   (tuna)
news.
I wi<u>sh Arkan</u>sas were closer to the ocean so we could surf.   (shark)

34. HINK PINK, HINKY PINKY & HINKITY PINKITY

Intro: Students often think that word study is boring. Here is a way to liven up the drill and practice for adjectives and syllabication.

Brain Link	Brain Processing Preference	Content Skill	Thinking Skill
Humor Novelty Practice Challenge	Verbal/Linguistic Analytic Individual, small groups	Rhyming Syllables Parts of speech Word meaning	Analysis Attributes

Materials: paper and pencil

Activity: Explain that a Hink Pink is a two-word phrase in which each of the words rhyme and is only one syllable. The two word phrases are usually adjective noun combinations.

Example: One syllable words that mean an unhappy father = a sad dad
A Hinky Pinky has rhyming words, each with two syllables.

Example: Two syllable words that mean a happy currant = merry berry
Have students create Hink Pinks related to a theme or topic of study.

Theme: Aviation	Answers
One syllable words that mean an evening airplane trip	night flight
One syllable words meaning a rational 747	sane plane
Two syllable words meaning an appropriate helicopter	proper chopper

Theme: School	Answers
An intelligent beginning	smart start
A noon-meal group	lunch bunch
A mean university	cruel school
A blackboard discussion	chalk talk
Cerebral overwork	brain strain
A superior exam	best test
A graphite etching	pencil stencil
A smarter author	brighter writer
A slender adolescent	lean teen
A sad or unhappy friend	glum chum
Malicious adolescent	mean teen
Temperate tot	mild child

35. HOMOGRAPHS

<u>Intro</u>: This activity gives students a fun and creative way to practice use of homographs.

Brain Link	Brain Processing Preference	Content Skill	Thinking Skill
Choice/Variety Novelty Humor Practice Challenge	Artistic Tactile Visual/Spatial Verbal/Linguistic	Word study Homographs	Comprehending Imagination Composing

<u>Materials</u>: Paper, markers, crayons or colored pencils

<u>Activity</u>: Homographs are words that sound the same and are spelled the same, but have different meanings. Ring and lock are examples of homographs.

What would a <u>lock</u> of hair and a <u>lock</u> that goes with a key look like? Illustrate the combination of the two meanings for the following homonyms.

 a ring for your finger

to ring a bell

lift: an elevator or to pick something up
stick: cling to something or part of a branch that has fallen
key: for lock or a piano key
pound: a place for stray animals or what you do with a hammer
ball: a toy that bounces or Cinderella's dance
match: two things that go together or what you strike to light a fire
park   put your car in a particular place or place with trees
coat: a thick covering of paint or a heavy jacket
punch: a fruit flavored drink or to hit with your fists

<u>Variation</u>: Students use the dictionary to find the meanings of the following homographs and then use both in a sentence.

bank	train	light	pop	kid
pitcher	bill	top	fly	bark
rose	sheet	leaves	trip	

36. HOMOPHONES

Intro: Homophones are words that are not spelled alike, but are pronounced the same. In this activity, students write and illustrate riddles that show the use of homophones.

Brain Link	Brain Processing Preference	Content Skill	Thinking Skill
Choice/Variety Novelty Humor Practice	Verbal/Linguistic Visual/Spatial Tactile Individual	Word study Homophones	Comprehending Imagination Composing Originality Attributes

Materials: paper and pencil

Activity: Homophones are words that sound alike but have a different spelling.
Write a short definition for 10 homonyms.
Example: To exist and a buzzing insect   <u>be</u>   <u>bee</u>
Choose your favorite two sets of homonyms. Write riddles and illustrate them.
Assemble a booklet of homonym riddles and illustrations.
Example: What did the passenger say to the travel agent when he got a great deal on a low-priced ticket to Europe?

What a fair fare!

Choose your favorite five sets and write antonym clues. For example: If the homophones are SAIL and SALE, the clues could be RAISE and LOWER.

37. HOW MANY WORDS FROM ONE?

Intro: Students will be surprised how many words they can find in another word. This activity promotes critical thinking and allows for friendly competition.

Brain Link	Brain Processing Preference	Content Skill	Thinking Skill
Novelty Challenge Pattern seeking	Verbal/Linguistic Visual/Spatial Analytic Individual Group	Word study Decoding Spelling Dictionary skills	Problem solving

Materials: paper and pencil

Activity:
Students make as many words as they can out of one main word. Use a word that relates to a unit theme or topic. Partners or small groups may want to compete to see who can find the greatest number of words.

Rules: No contractions, no proper nouns, no foreign words, no slang, and no hyphenated words.

alphabet

There are 30 four-letter words, 10 five-letter words, and one six-letter word.

Four- letter words
Abet, able, bale, bath, beat, belt, beta, hale, halt, hate, heal, heap, heat, help, late, lath, leap, pale, pate, path, peal, peat, pelt, plat, plea, tale, tape, teal
Five-letter words
Abate, alpha, bathe, bleat, lathe, petal, plate, pleat, table
Six-letter words
Palate

38. I HAVE; WHO HAS

Intro: This activity teaches students to "think on their feet" and change gears quickly. It is an active way to review material for testing.

Brain Link	Brain Processing Preference	Content Skill	Thinking Skill
Attention/focus Practice Feedback Activate prior knowledge Social interaction	Verbal/Linguistic Auditory Tactile Group	Vocabulary Listening	Flexibility Risk taking Cause and effect

Materials: question and answer cards

Example: **Middle School Literature** This game can be constructed for any subject or theme. Cut apart the boxes and distribute randomly to your students. The student with the starred card begins the game by reading the "Who has" portion of the card. Students will need to listen carefully to respond correctly. The following example is based on the book Walkabout by James Vance Marshall.

I HAVE South Carolina. **WHO HAS … When did the first Europeans settled in Australia?	I HAVE 200 years ago. WHO HAS… the European explorer who found Australia?
I HAVE Captain Cook. WHO HAS the official language for the Australian continent?	I HAVE English. WHO HAS where Peter and Mary were lost?
I HAVE Northern Territory. WHO HAS the Aborigine word for "girl"?	I HAVE lubra. WHO HAS where Uncle Keith lives?
I HAVE Adelaide. WHO HAS a journey of 6 to 8 months undertaken by bush boys as a test of manhood?	I HAVE walkabout. WHO HAS the point of view of this book?
I HAVE 3rd person omniscient. WHO HAS one of the themes of this book?	I HAVE racial and cultural stereotyping causes misconceptions. WHO HAS why the Bush Boy felt pity for the Mary and Peter?
I HAVE Mary and Peter were helpless. WHO HAS what the Aborigine people were predominantly devoted to waging war with?	I HAVE life and death. WHO HAS the original home of the children?

39. INSIDE OUTSIDE CIRCLES

Intro: This activity is a format to focus large group discussions and actively involve all students. It gives students the opportunity to explain and clarify issues and/or opinions or can be used as a form of review.

Brain Link	Brain Processing Preference	Content Skill	Thinking Skill
Activate prior knowledge Social interaction Feedback Relevance Practice Multiple memory pathways Create safe environment	Bodily/Kinesthetic Class or large group	Anything for review or to activate prior knowledge	Risk taking Focusing skills Brainstorming Attributes Unlimited

Materials: none

Activity: Students divide into two equal groups, and form two circles; one group stands inside the other. Students face each other. The teacher poses a question for the inside circle students to answer to their outside circle partner. After these students have answered the question, the teacher gives a signal (a whistle or chime) and asks the outside circle to take two steps to their left finding a new partner. The teacher poses a different question for the outside circle to answer. Note: The teacher has the choice of who will answer the question; either inside, outside, or both, if there will be debate between the two, and how often to rotate the circles.

Options: Each partner answers the question the teacher poses. Opinion and summary questions work best for this option.

Variation: Use this activity as a "Getting to Know You" activity or for student interviews where students share information about themselves.

40. JEOPARDY

Intro: The word *game* is synonymous with *fun!* This answer-question format is a refreshing and motivating way to review lessons and information that will be tested. Be prepared for a more active learning environment with the bit of competition Jeopardy creates!

Brain Link	Brain Processing Preference	Content Skill	Thinking Skill
Social interaction Practice Feedback Novelty Attention	Verbal/Linguistic Interpersonal Analytic Tactile Individual, groups	All	Comprehension Analysis Evaluation Risk taking

Materials: paper and pencil, Jeopardy chart

To make the Jeopardy chart, divide information into five categories with each category divided into five questions that increase in difficulty. Add point values to each square.

Activity: Divide the class into two teams.

A student from one team chooses a category and difficulty level. That answer is read, and the student supplies the question and points are awarded or withheld. The student who questions the answer correctly selects the next category and point amount. If a wrong answer is given, the other team has thirty seconds to answer. If they cannot answer, neither team receives points.

Variation: Have students use their Fact File information (activity Number 25) to write the Jeopardy board questions and assign point values.

Example: Literary Terms-20 points. In the story, early references to fear and evil are examples of this technique. (What is foreshadowing?)

Characters	Plot	Trivia	Vocabulary	Literary terms
10	10	10	10	10
20	20	20	20	20
30	30	30	30	30
40	40	40	40	40
50	50	50	50	50

Category titles:

Nouns	Verbs	Adjectives	Adverbs	Prepositions
Battles	Heroes	Losses	Event Order	Reasons for War

41. JIGSAW JUXTAPOSITION

Intro: Jigsaw is an exciting alternative to textbook reading and teacher lecture. In this activity every student teaches something and is therefore accountable for a portion of the information.

Brain Link	Brain Processing Preference	Content Skill	Thinking Skill
Social interaction Practice Feedback	Verbal/Linguistic Visual Tactile Individual, small groups	All	Problem solving Comprehension Analysis Evaluation Creating Designing

Activity: Divide the class into "home" teams of three students and assign each student a number from 1 to 3. Give each team member one part of a topic to research. Each team member joins with other members from other teams with the same number and topic. All the 1s get together, all the 2s get together, etc. These specialized groups research their topics and think of the best ways to teach their home teams using a visual representation or a prop. Then they return to their home teams and teach all the other members about the topic. They learn the information presented by others in the group as well.

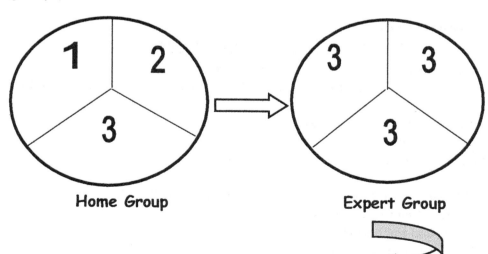

Home Group   Expert Group

Members return to home group to teach each other.

42. JOKES and RIDDLES

Intro: Everyone loves to laugh. Jokes and riddles stretch student thinking and promote positive interactions in the classroom setting.

Brain Link	Brain Processing Preference	Content Skill	Thinking Skill
Humor Trigger emotions Social interaction Novelty Challenge Variety	Verbal/Linguistic Interpersonal Analytic Individual, pairs, groups	All	Attributes Complexity Flexibility Originality Risk taking Analyzing Synthesizing

Materials: paper and pencil

Activity: Have students write knock knock jokes using vocabulary terms or spelling words.

Examples: States and Cities

Knock Knock.
Who's there?
Iowa.
Iowa who?
Iowa you a dollar.

Knock Knock.
Who's there?
Missouri.
Missouri who?
Missouri loves company.

Knock Knock
Who's there?
Tex.
Tex who?
Tex two to tango.

Question Answer Riddles

Words, Letters, and Grammar

Q: What is the difference between a cat and a comma?
    A: One has the paws before the claws and the other has the clause before the pause.
Q: What letter is never found in the alphabet?
    A: The one you put in the mailbox.
Q: In what way are the letter A and noon the same?
    A: Both are in the middle of DAY.
Q: Why should everyone go to sleep after drinking a cup of tea?
    A: Because when the T is gone, NIGHT is NIGH.
Q: What do shoes and the blues have in common?
    A: They both have sole/soul.
Q: What do books and stop signs have in common?
    A: They are both red/read.

43. JOURNALS

Intro: Journal writing promotes independent reflection and allows students to reflect on meaningful personal experiences, opinions, and ideas. Journaling encourages students to become more aware of what is happening to them and why they feel the way they do.

Brain Link	Brain Processing Preference	Content Skill	Thinking Skill
Reflection Relevance Multiple memory pathways	Verbal/Linguistic Interpersonal Individual	All	Analysis Synthesizing Evaluation Composing Observing

Materials: paper or notebook and pencil

Activity: Journals can be used every day or several times a week and are usually kept in a separate notebook. The following prompts are designed for students to write down their personal ideas, feelings, thoughts, observations, and opinions.

Examples: Usually when I say "I can't," I really mean "_____." Instead I could say "_____" because....

If every ending is really a new beginning, I am just now starting to _____ for myself because....

Intellectual risk-taking requires me to be honest with myself about _____ because...

The most important goal I have for myself this year is _____ because...

The problem that bothers me the most is _____ because...

Other people see me being successful at _____ because... But I feel most successful when _____ because...

Usually when I feel like quitting it's because.... The thing that keeps me going is _____ because...

I wish I had the knowledge to _____ because.....

I'm thankful to be living at this time because... The world is thankful I'm here because...

The one thing I'd most like to learn this year is _____ because....

I like tasks that let me _____ because....

To me winning is....

I have learned appreciation for...

44. KETCHUP and MUSTARD

Intro: Consolidating new learning is fun when you add a little ketchup or mustard! This activity gives students an opportunity to talk with another student about relevant information.

Brain Link	Brain Processing Preference	Content Skill	Thinking Skill
Relevance Activate prior knowledge Sifting Social interaction	Verbal/Linguistic Interpersonal Auditory Pairs	All	Metacognition Summarizing Point of view Elaboration Analysis

Materials: none

Activity: In this activity, students will need a partner. Student A (ketchup) gives a summary of the information learned in a lesson to Student B (mustard). Switch roles.

KETCHUP ONLY

"Ketchup" can also be a day or a class period when students are allowed to work on any projects that need to be completed or a class time to 'catch up.'

45. KINESTHETIC NAME GAME

Intro: This name game is actively engaging, exciting and a fun way for students to get to know one another. It is great first day of school activity.

Brain Link	Brain Processing Preference	Content Skill	Thinking Skill
Create safe environment Trigger emotions Social interaction Mind body link Humor Multiple memory pathways	Bodily/Kinesthetic Whole class, small groups	Listening Following directions	Observation Attributes Problem solving Risk taking

Materials: none

Activity: Students stand in a circle. A student steps into the circle and introduces him or herself and performs some action. All students respond with, "Hi, (student's name)" and repeat the action. The second student steps into circle, introduces him/herself and performs a different action. The rest of the student respond with "Hi, the second student's name and action, and then repeats the first student's name and action. An example: "Hi, I'm Jack" and claps his hands twice. All students respond, "Hi, Jack" and clap their hands twice. Second student, "Hi, I'm Sandy" and wiggles. The rest of the class responds with "Hi, Sandy," and wiggles, "Hi, Jack," and claps hands twice. This continues until all students have introduced themselves and performed an action.

46. KWL

Intro: KWL is a strategy that models active thinking. This strategy helps the students determine prior knowledge and requires them to consider needed information on a topic.

Brain Link	Brain Processing Preference	Content Skill	Thinking Skill
Focus Relevance Activate prior knowledge	Verbal/Linguistic Visual Individual, pair, small groups	All	Curiosity Questioning Composing Research Metacognition

Materials: paper and pencil

Activity: Make a chart or booklet divided into three sections. Label each section with a K, W, or L. Students write in the columns what they know about a topic, and what they want to find out about the topic. After completing the study, students write what they learned in the L column.
K = What do I KNOW?
W = WHAT do I want to learn? WHAT questions need to be asked?
L = What did I LEARN?

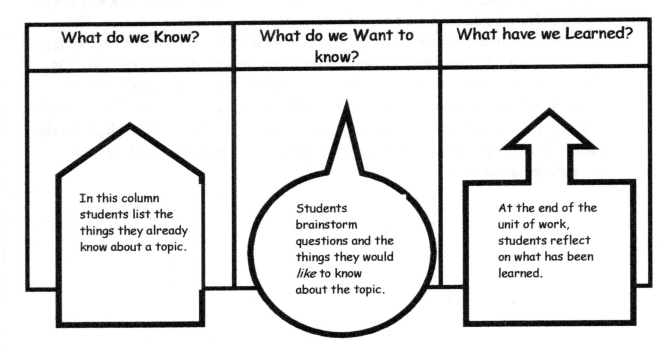

What do we Know?	What do we Want to know?	What have we Learned?
In this column students list the things they already know about a topic.	Students brainstorm questions and the things they would *like* to know about the topic.	At the end of the unit of work, students reflect on what has been learned.

47. LINE UPS

Intro: This activity creates a spirit of cooperation and interdependence. It is excellent for students who already know each other.

Brain Link	Brain Processing Preference	Content Skill	Thinking Skill
Social interaction Pattern seeking	Verbal/Linguistic Visual Tactile Whole class, large groups	Non verbal communication skills	Problem solving

Materials: none

Activity: Students line up in order of some aspect of a theme. Many lineups can be done in complete silence, using only non-verbal communication.

Example: Students draw cards that contain a picture or a word related to a theme and line up in alphabetical order of the pictures or words.

Variation: Instead of using a content material, students can line up by birthdays, height, first letters of their names in alphabetical order, or shoe size.

48. LOGIC PUZZLES

Intro: Logic puzzles are fun and stretch student thinking. Link logic puzzles to content to teach facts, vocabulary, parts of speech, cause and effect, or reinforce research skills. When students are solving logic puzzles, they are at the analysis level of Bloom's Taxonomy. When they are writing logic puzzles, they are at the synthesis level of Bloom's Taxonomy.

Brain Link	Brain Processing Preference	Content Skill	Thinking Skill
Novelty Challenge Practice Variety Pattern seeking	Verbal/Linguistic Logical/Mathematical Analytic Individual, pairs, small groups	All	Analysis Attributes Problem solving Inferring Cause and effect

Materials: paper and pencil

Activity: How to write a logic problem linked to content

1. Decide on A solution or basic facts.
   Margie = first
   Jimmy = second
   Lawrence = third
2. Make a grid and begin writing your clues. Mark the grid as you write each clue.
3. Scramble your clues and work the problem with a clean grid.
4. Once you are certain your problem is correct, recopy it.

The following is an example of a logic puzzle linked to the theme of aviation.

	THRUST	LIFT	DRAG	GRAVITY
CHRIS				
DAVID				
RAMSEY				
SHELLY				

Christopher, Ramsey, David and Shelly all missed one definition on their pilot's exam. Each missed a different term. The terms were thrust, drag, lift and gravity, but not necessarily in that order. Which term did each person miss?

1. Christopher and David understood thrust and lift.
2. Shelly sat by Christopher during the exam.
3. Ramsey thought that lift was a downward force.
4. David studied two months for his exam.
5. The person who sat by Shelly responded correctly to a question on gravity.

Proof: x means *answered correctly;* 0 *means answered incorrectly*

1. Chris and David understood thrust and lift

	THRUST	LIFT	DRAG	GRAVITY
CHRIS	X	X		
DAVID	X	X		
RAMSEY				
SHELLY				

2. Shelly and Chris sat together
3. Ramsey thought that lift was a downward force.

	THRUST	LIFT	DRAG	GRAVITY
CHRIS	X	X		
DAVID	X	X		
RAMSEY	X	0	X	X
SHELLY	0	X	X	X

4. David studied for two months
5. Person by Shelly understood gravity

	THRUST	LIFT	DRAG	GRAVITY
CHRIS	X	X	0	X
DAVID	X	X	X	0
RAMSEY	X	0	X	X
SHELLY	0	X	X	X

SOLUTION:

Chris = drag   Ramsey = lift
Shelly = thrust   David = gravity

Oldest and Tallest

Melissa is younger than Natalie and is older and shorter than Jason.
Natalie is taller and younger than Ken, but Ken is taller than Jason.
List the ages of the four people in order, starting with the oldest.
List the heights of the four people in order, starting with the tallest.

49. MIME AND MODEL IT!

Intro: This activity is an excellent way of giving students an opportunity to be creative in demonstrating understanding and practicing performance skills. Students may choose to work individually, in pairs or in threes to create their own scenarios to illustrate class lessons or concepts.

Brain Link	Brain Processing Preference	Content Skill	Thinking Skill
Mind/body link Multiple pathways Social interaction Humor Attention	Bodily/ Kinesthetic Interpersonal Visual Partner, groups	Nonverbal communication Cooperation Context clues	Comprehension Analysis Synthesis Risk taking Imagination

Materials: Content related concepts, vocabulary, or spelling words

Activity: Write 10 to 20 words, phrases, or concepts on note cards and place them in a basket or box. Divide the class into teams and play "Mime and Model It" in the same way you would play charades. A few examples of words for the theme of flight could be gravity, speed of light, lift, drag, Fly Me to the Moon, Rocket Man, safe landing, or May the Force Be with You.

Students communicate by miming and use of non- verbal convention.

Examples: Famous people
Inventions and inventors
Book titles and authors
Games and entertainment
Law, order, citizenship
Nursery rhymes
Grammar and punctuation
Idioms
Literary elements

50. MIND MAPS

Intro: Mind Maps are any kind of visual picture reflecting students' knowledge. They are a creative pattern of connected ideas. Mind maps appeal to both sides of the brain. The left side processes words and the right side processes colors, symbols, pictures, and relationships.

Brain Link	Brain Processing Preference	Content Skill	Thinking Skill
Activate prior knowledge Multiple memory pathways Reflection Evaluation Relevance	Verbal/Linguistic Visual/Spatial Intrapersonal Tactile Artistic Global Analytic	All	Can involve all

Materials: paper, pencil and markers

Activity: Mind mapping is a creative way for students to generate ideas, record learning, or plan a new project. Creating a mind map helps students to identify clearly and creatively what they are planning or what they have learned.

Students draw a mind map using words, pictures, and color.

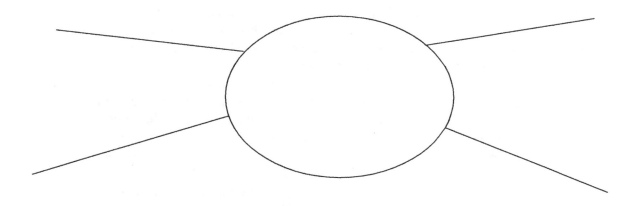

51. MINI UNIT

Intro: Independent projects offer choice and variety to students. A mini unit, using Bloom's Taxonomy, can be designed to fit on 8½ by 11 heavy paper or on file folders. Laminate each sheet or folder for easy storage.

Brain Link	Brain Processing Preference	Content Skill	Thinking Skill
Choice Variety Practice	Verbal/Linguistic Logical/Mathematical Intrapersonal Artistic Analytic Individual	Independent learning for all areas	Composing Organizing Problem solving

Materials: Student has the choice of materials to design creative and original products for each activity.

Examples:

Famous Women

Knowledge:	Make a fact file about your famous woman.
Comprehension:	Write a report using the information in your fact file.
Application:	Design an informational poster. It should point out reasons why she should be remembered.
Analysis:	Using a Venn diagram, compare and contrast a woman from a different time period, or two famous women from the same period.
Synthesis:	Write and illustrate a newspaper or one issue of your own Women's Magazine.
Evaluation:	Set criteria for your newspaper and/or magazine and rate your work. Ask another student to rate your work. Compare the results.

My School and Me

Knowledge:	Write a definition of 'A School" and put it on a poster with illustrations.
Comprehension:	Make up a word search of at least 10 words related to school.
Application:	What question would you ask your grandparent or an elderly person to find out about school when they were children? Write a letter to the person you have chosen, asking them your questions.
Analysis:	Design a questionnaire to find out your classmates' favorite activities at school. Present your findings on a graph and explain it to the class.
Synthesis:	Imagine you and your classmates were given the job of running the school cafeteria. Make a brochure to advertise the food and services offered and hours the cafeteria will operate.
Evaluation:	Give five reasons why you think everyone should have to go to school. List them in order of importance and be ready to support your ranking.

52. MIX FREEZE PAIR

<u>Intro</u>: The brain can only sustain concentrated attention for short periods of time. Higher levels of thinking are stifled when students are asked to stay seated too long. This is great activity to get students standing and moving to review material.

Brain Link	Brain Processing Preference	Content Skill	Thinking Skill
Practice Feedback Social interaction Sifting	Interpersonal Auditory Whole class	All	Summarizing Analysis Risk taking

<u>Materials</u>: none

<u>Activity</u>: Ask students to stand and move around the room. When the teacher says, "Freeze," students stop, make eye contact with another student, and pair up. The teacher can ask students to state one thing they have learned in the lesson, summarize a theory, describe a character, or tell something personal. Repeat and find a new partner. This activity can be used for reviewing a topic, spelling words, vocabulary definitions, etc.

<u>Variation</u>: Play music while students are milling around. When the music stops, they must find a partner.

53. MNEMONICS

Intro: Mnemonics are memory tools that utilize the principle of association. These devices come in a variety of forms, such as a jingle or a rhyme, an acronym, peg system, or a catch phrase to aid memory. When students link prior knowledge and experiences to new information, they are more likely to keep or store the information and retrieve it more easily when needed.

Brain Link	Brain Processing Preference	Content Skill	Thinking Skill
Pattern seeking	Verbal/Linguistic	All	Composing
Meaning making	Auditory		Analysis
Challenge	Analytic		Synthesis
Novelty	Individual, pairs, triads		Originality

Activity: Teach students about mnemonics and have them create one to remember information for a test, a speech, or a spelling rule.

Rhymes The number of days in each month of the year:

Thirty days hath September,	Excepting February alone:
April, June, and November;	Which hath but twenty-eight, in fine,
All the rest have thirty-one	Till leap year gives it twenty-nine

Spelling rules: I before E except after C. And "weird" is just weird.
Or when sounded like "A" as in neighbor and weigh.

Catch phrases: "Fall back –spring forward" for time changes
There is a "rat" in separate. Your principal is your PAL

Spelling mnemonics: RHYTHM
Rhythm Helps Your Two Hips Move

List order mnemonics: Order of taxonomy in biology:
(Kingdom, Phylum, Class, Order, Family, Genus, Species)
Kids Prefer Candy Over Fried Green Spinach
The 4 Oceans
(Indian, Arctic, Atlantic, Pacific) I Am A Person
The Great Lakes (Huron, Ontario, Michigan, Erie and Superior)
HOMES

Colors in the rainbow in order: **ROY G BIV** Red, Orange, Yellow, Green, Blue, Indigo, Violet

Order of operations in algebra: Please Excuse My Dear Aunt Sally
Parentheses, Exponents, Multiplication, Division, Addition,
Subtraction

Peg System: A peg list only has to be memorized one time and can then be used over and over every time a list of items needs to be memorized. It works by pre-memorizing a list of words that are easy to associate with the numbers they represent (1 to 10). To memorize a list of arbitrary objects, associate each one with the appropriate peg.

1-sun	5-hive	9-line
2-shoe	6-bricks	10-pen
3-tree	7-heaven	
4-door	8-plate	

54. MOCK TRIAL

Intro: Students need to learn how to look at situations from more than one viewpoint or perspective. This is a life long skill that encourages discernment and reflection.

Brain Link	Brain Processing Preference	Content Skill	Thinking Skill
Trigger emotions Novelty Challenge Refection and evaluation Social interaction Relevance	Verbal/Linguistic Interpersonal Bodily/Kinesthetic Analytic Small groups	All	Problem solving Analysis Synthesis Point of view Organizing skills Sequencing Cause and effect Fact and opinion Brainstorming Risk taking

Materials: Student handouts on trial procedures.

Activity: Students work in groups of four to prepare, rehearse, and present a mock trial related to a topic. They will need a lawyer for the prosecution, a lawyer for the defense, a judge, a defendant, witnesses, and possibly a jury.

Examples:

Fairy Tales

Goldilocks and the Three Bears criminal trespass, criminal damage to property and robbery of food

Hansel and Gretel murder

Peter Rabbit criminal trespass and robbery

Sport Unit

An athlete who has been accused of using steroids

Literature

Children living in a library (criminal trespass)

War criminals

Illegal use of magical powers

55. MYSTERIOUS MESSAGES

Intro: Students love a mystery and this activity will engage their curiosity. Codes can be used for spelling words, vocabulary definitions, and as puzzles in literature. A cipher is made up of two parts – a general system and a specific key.

A.	B.	C.	D.	E.	F.	G.	H.	I.	J.	K.	L.	M.	N.	O.	P.	Q.	R.	S.	T.	U.	V.	W.	X.	Y.	Z.
L	M	N	O	P	Q	R	S	T	U	V	W	X	Y	Z	A	B	C	D	E	F	G	H	I	J	K

NDJ PGT RAPKPG!   Answer: You are clever!

Brain Link	Brain Processing Preference	Content Skill	Thinking Skill
Pattern seeking Meaning making Challenge Novelty	Mathematical/Logical Verbal/Linguistic Analytic Individual, pairs	All	Problem solving Analysis Finding patterns

Materials: Paper and pencil

Activity: Students can make cipher scramblers by cutting two different sized circles from card paper and writing the alphabet on the outside edges. Place a brad in the center and the code will change as you spin the inside smaller wheel.

Variation: Columns of Four

First, write out your message and divide it into groups of four letters. If your message is short, fill in with misleading letters. Second, print the letters vertically in columns of four. Third, recopy the letters as they appear horizontally.

Good luck on your test

G   L   O   U   S
O   U   N   R   T
O   C   Y   T   O
D   K   O   E   O

3. GLOUS OUNRT OCYTO DKOE

Variation: Name it code

When using this code, hide the message in the initials within a list of names.

   Mary H. Latham
   Barry E. Spots
   James L. Joyce
   Jake P. Rose   Answer: HELP

56. NAME GAME ALLITERATIVE ADJECTIVES

Intro: Alliterative adjectives amplify articulation and accent anticipation among aspiring apprentices. This activity requires students to assign a positive characteristic or adjective to their first name such as Marvelous Mary or Jolly Jake. The adjective must begin with the same sound as their first name (alliteration).

Brain Link	Brain Processing Preference	Content Skill	Thinking Skill
Novelty Humor Social interaction Humor Attention Multiple memory pathways	Intrapersonal Interpersonal Verbal/Linguistic Tactile Auditory Group	Adjectives Alliteration Listening Following directions	Attributes Imagination Risk taking

Materials: none

Activity: Teachers introduce this game in the following way:

"My name is Mrs. Smith (note the teacher is the only person who uses last name). I am a very happy person so the alliterative adjective I am going to use to describe me is 'smiley'. Therefore, I am Mrs. Smiley Smith." Mrs. Smiley Smith shakes the hand of a student and introduces herself. That student replies with, "Glad to meet you. I am Courageous Courtney." Student number one turns to student number two, shakes his hand, and introduces himself and the teacher. Students introduce themselves and introduce those students who have already participated, ending with the teacher.

Example:

"Hi, I'm Lucky Larry, and I'd like you to meet my friends, Jolly Jake, Marvelous Mary, Super Sarah, Delightful Dan, Gregarious Grace, and Mrs. Smiley Smith."

The last student shakes hands with the teacher and names all the students in the class. Then the teacher walks over to the first student and shakes his/her hand and says, "Hi, I'm Mrs. Smiley Smith, and I'd like you to meet the class." The teacher names all the students in the class.

Variation: Students create new names using their initials. An example would be Janet Smith becomes "Just Silly". Students can add their names during introductions, Just Silly, Janet Smith, or Daringly Great, David Gooding.

57. NEWSPAPER REPORTER

Intro: Newspaper Reporter is a great first day of school activity. It can also be used to create reports.

Brain Link	Brain Processing Preference	Content Skill	Thinking Skill
Challenge Humor Choice Variety Relevance	Verbal/Linguistic Logical/Mathematical Analytic Artistic Individual Individual, pairs, small groups	Writing Research Grammar Summarizing	Synthesis Designing Composing Complexity Elaboration Fact and opinion Imagination Point of view Integrating skills Originality

Materials: paper and pencil

Activity: Students introduce each other to the rest of the class after interviewing a partner with Who, What, Where, When and How questions.

Variation: Students prepare features of a newspaper based around a particular theme.

Example: a fantasy novel

> **Headlines**: *Criminal Escapes! Hogwarts guarded by Dementors!*
> The report should tell Who, What, When, Where, and sometimes Why. If the facts haven't been proven, students should use the term 'alleged."
> **Article/reports**: details of escape and criminal profile
> **Interviews using question and answer formant**: Interview Professor Dumbledorf or students at Hogwarts
> **Advertisements**: for Diagon Alley proprietors for personalized wands
> **Sports reports**: Quidditch matches
> **Crosswords and horoscopes**
> **TV programs for a day**
> **Weather forecast**
> **Editorial**

58. NO VOWELS

Intro: Vowels do not exist in the land of MT (Empty). Try this activity with vocabulary and spelling words or phrases and sentences.

Brain Link	Brain Processing Preference	Content Skill	Thinking Skill
Novelty Challenge Pattern seeking	Verbal/Linguistic Logical/Mathematical Analytic Individual	All	Problem solving

Materials: paper and pencil

Activity: Identify the words, phrases, characters, titles, or quotes by filling in the missing vowels.

Knwldg s pwr.   Knowledge is power.

Hrry Pttr   Harry Potter

tlvsn   television

Variation: Write a limerick or a paragraph with basic information without any vowels. Have students write the information after finding the missing vowels.

```
    A   CH_ _RF_L   _LD   B_ _R   _T   TH_   Z_O
    C_ _LD   _LW_YS   F_ND   S_M_TH_NG   T_   D_,
        WH_N   _T   B_R_D   H_M,   Y_ _   KN_W
        T_   W_LK   T_   _ND   FR_,
    H_   R_V_RS_D   _T   _ND   W_LK_D   FR_   _ND   T_.
```

A cheerful old bear at the zoo
Could always find something to do,
When it bored him, you know
To walk to and fro,
He reversed it and walked fro and to.

59. NUMBER REPORT

Intro: Students often think that writing a report is boring. Here is a way to liven it up. The Number Report framework provides an organizational structure for reporting researched information.

Brain Link	Brain Processing Preference	Content Skill	Thinking Skill
Novelty Challenge Practice Variety	Verbal/Linguistic Artistic Analytic Individual	Writing Summarizing Paraphrasing Graphic organizers	Analysis Cause and effect Compare/contract Classify/sort Originality

Materials: student choice

Activity:

AUSTRALIA

10   Ten important numbers in the demographics and geography of Australia, including areas, populations, lengths of rivers, and lakes, and coastlines.

9   Nine key dates in Australia's history, beginning with the First Fleet. *Time line and facts.*

8   Eight unusual animals and/or plants found in Australia. *Illustrate.*

7   Seven famous Australians-past and present. *Design a chart or matrix to organize information.*

6   Six key facts about Aboriginal culture. *(Past and present)*

5   Five famous tourist attractions. *Brochure* or *PowerPoint*

4   Four differences between Australian and American kids: education, driving, dating, etc. *(Use columns)*

3   Three Australian foods popular with the local population and tourists.

2   Two reasons why you think Australia is called the "Lucky Country."

1   One significant observation about Australia. *Paragraph*

60. OUGHTOGRAPHS

Intro: This activity allows for creative design and analysis in any subject.

Brain Link	Brain Processing Preference	Content Skill	Thinking Skill
Novelty Challenge Trigger emotions Humor	Visual/Spatial Intrapersonal Artistic Analytic Individual	All	Attributes Analysis Synthesis Elaboration Imagination

Materials: paper and markers

Activity:
How do you think story characters 'ought to' sign their names? Be creative and design oughtographs for several of the main characters in the story.

Fang
(( ))

Variation: Create oughtographs for authors, scientists, mathematicians, actors, or yourself.

61. PAIR INTERVIEWS

Intro: This activity builds empathy, or putting yourself in someone else's shoes.

Brain Link	Brain Processing Preference	Content Skill	Thinking Skill

Relevance
Trigger emotions
Social
  interaction
	Interpersonal
	Intrapersonal
	Verbal/Linguistic
	Analytic
	Pairs
		Speaking
		Listening
		Following
		  directions
			Cause/effect
			Risk taking
			Summarizing

Materials: none

Activity: In this activity, students work with a partner and take turns interviewing each other using in-depth questions provided by the teacher.

Example: Tell about a time when you did something for someone else.

            Tell about a time when you were tempted to give up but managed to stick it out.

62. PAIRED PROBLEM SOLVING

Intro: Critical thinking is more fun with a partner.

Brain Link	Brain Processing Preference	Content Skill	Thinking Skill

Challenge
Social
  interactions
Practice
Reflection
Feedback
Multiple memory
  pathways
	Logical/Mathematical
	Verbal/Linguistic
	Analytic
	Auditory
	Pairs
		Listening
		Comprehension
		Sequence
			Problem solving
			Analysis
			Find patterns
			Risk taking

Materials: paper and pencil

Activity: Students pair up and solve a problem. One student is the listener and the other student is the problem solver.

Instructions:

Listeners will continually check accuracy and actively work along with the problem solver. Stop the problem solver and ask for an explanation if you do not understand or agree. When you identify an error, point it out, but do not give the correct solution. Demand constant vocalization; this is the only way to communicate and monitor thinking.

Examples: Alphabet

Which letter is as far away from K in the alphabet as J is from G?

       1. K   2. M   3. N   4. G   5. I

Thinking: Indicate the position of the letter in the word DIVERGENT, which is the seventh letter in the alphabet.

A. first	C. third	E. sixth	G. eighth
B. second	D. fourth	F. seventh	H. ninth

Foreign Pollution

The words "mae radey quiid" in another language mean, "pollution is serious," but not necessarily in that order. In the same language "sieer mae tisd" means "stop serious littering" and "de sieer quiid" means, "help stop pollution". Which word means pollution?

Directions

If you are facing east and turn left, then make an about-face and turn left again, in which direction are you facing? a. east   b. north   c. west   d. south   e. south

Answers: N, sixth, quid, east

63. PALINDROMES OR BACKWARDS AND FOREWORDS

Intro: Palindromes are words or expressions that are spelled the same forward and backward.

Brain Link	Brain Processing Preference	Content Skill	Thinking Skill
Novelty Practice Pattern seeking Humor	Verbal/Linguistic Analytic Individual	Dictionary skills Word meaning Context clues	Problem solving Finding patterns Curiosity

Materials: paper and pencil

Activity: Students find palindromes that relate to a theme or definition. Examples of palindromes are dad and rotor.

Find a palindrome that means midday.   NOON

Find a palindrome that means looks.   SEES

Find a palindrome that means instrument for detecting airplanes. RADAR

Find a palindrome that means the sound made by a horn.   TOOT

Find a palindrome that means an Eskimo boat.   KAYAK

Find a palindrome that means allows us to see.   EYE

Find a palindrome that means the sound a bird makes.   PEEP

Find a palindrome that means document showing ownership of land. DEED

64. PEOPLE SEARCHES

<u>Intro</u>: This scavenger hunt is for classmates, not objects. Students get moving right away. People searches foster team building. Survey the class about each item to stimulate interest.

Brain Link	Brain Processing Preference	Content Skill	Thinking Skill
Create safe environment Social interaction Novelty	Verbal/Linguistic Interpersonal Auditory Global Whole class	All	Risk taking Point of view Classify Attributes Observe Ranking Finding patterns

<u>Materials</u>: paper and pencil

<u>Activity</u>: Devise 6 to 12 descriptive statements to complete the phrase: "Find someone who has . . ." Students find one person in the group who fits each description or can answer a question. Have that person sign his or her name in the signature box. For example in a unit on the *Circus* students might be asked to find someone who:

♦ Can juggle
♦ Can explain the differences between an African and Indian elephant
♦ Has swung on a jungle gym trapeze

<u>Variation</u>: At the beginning of the school year write a People Search that includes statements that identify personal information. Have students answer the questions first and then find someone with the same answer. *Find someone who...*

♦ Has the same birthday as you
♦ Is left handed
♦ Can demonstrate their favorite sport
♦ Has the same color eyes as you
♦ Has the same favorite music group or singer as you
♦ Has the same favorite school subject

This is a great mixer and icebreaker and can be used with any class size.

65. PMI ASSESSMENT/EVALUATION

Intro: The brain needs time to think and reflect on new information. A PMI is a great strategy to use during and after students have read, listened, or experimented with learning material.

Brain Link	Brain Processing Preference	Content Skill	Thinking Skill
Reflection and evaluation Pattern seeking/meaning making Relevance	Verbal/Linguistic Intrapersonal Tactile Individual	All	Evaluation Fact and opinion Cause and effect

Materials: paper and pencil

Activity:
A PMI is a thinking strategy proposed by Edward de Bono. Students are asked to list Pluses or positive aspects, Minus or negative aspects, and I or interesting aspects of an idea, issue, or plan related to a theme.

Example: Topic: Animals
Do a PMI on animal testing.
Do a PMI on exhibiting animals at the zoo or circus.
Do a PMI on the strategy PMI.

PLUS ➕	MINUS ➖	INTERESTING ❓
benefits/strengths/ positives/good things	deficiencies/weaknesses/ minuses/negatives	attention-grabbing/out of the ordinary/appealing

66. RAP IT

Intro: Brain research tells us that the more ways that information enters the brain, the more learning will stick. This activity helps to cement learning by using music, chanting, and novelty.

Brain Link	Brain Processing Preference	Content Skill	Thinking Skill
Pattern seeking Novelty Challenge Social interaction	Musical/Rhythmic Verbal/Linguistic Bodily/Kinesthetic Auditory Analytic Individual, pairs, groups	All	Imagination Sequencing Summarizing Elaboration Analysis Risk taking

Materials: paper and pencil

Activity: Either in groups or individually, students prepare, rehearse, and perform a rap song related to a theme. This activity can be used for grammar, antonyms, synonyms, number facts, rules, concepts, presidents, etc.

Example Division Rap:

> I'm Mrs. Smith and I'm on the scene
>
> With a division rap that's really mean.
>
> It goes DIVIDE, MULTIPLY, SUBTRACT, AND BRING DOWN.
>
> I said DIVIDE, MULTIPLY, SUBTRACT, AND BRING DOWN.

67. S.C.A.M.P.E.R.

Intro: Scamper is a concept created by Bob Eberle. This strategy is designed to enhance students' creative abilities and provide a framework for brainstorming a greater number of ideas.

Brain Link	Brain Processing Preference	Content Skill	Thinking Skill
Novelty Variety Humor Challenge	Verbal/Linguistic Global Analytic Individual, pairs, groups	All	Synthesis Analysis Curiosity Attributes Flexibility Originality Complexity

Materials: Copy of SCAMPER model

Substitute   Who else instead? What else instead? Other ingredient?
Other material, color, function? Other power? Other place?

Combine   How about a blend, an alloy, an ensemble?

Combine units? Combine purposes? Combine appeals?
Adapt   What else is like this? What other idea does this
suggest? Other purpose? Does past offer parallel? What could I
copy? Conform? Adjust?

Modify   New twist? Change meaning, color, motion, sound, odor, form,
  Magnify   shape? Transform?
  Minify   What to add? More time? Greater frequency? Higher? Longer?
Thicker? Subtract? Divide?

Put to other uses

New ways to use as is? Other uses if modified?
Other places to use? Other people to reach?
Eliminate   What to subtract? Smaller? Condense? Miniature? Lower?
Shorter? Lighter? Omit? Streamline? Understate?

Rearrange / Reverse

Interchange components? Other pattern? Other layout?
Other sequence? Transpose cause and effect? Change pace?
Transpose positive and negative? How about opposites? Turn it
backward? Turn it upside down? Reverse roles?

68. SIX HATS

Intro: Sticking to the topic during discussions can be difficult for many students. The Six Thinking Hats strategy, developed by Edward de Bono, provides a structure for thinking and keeps kids on track.

Brain Link	Brain Processing Preference	Content Skill	Thinking Skill
Attention/Focus Practice Activate prior knowledge Challenge Relevance	Verbal/Linguistic Logical Global Analytic Auditory Small groups, whole class	All	Analysis Problem solving Synthesis

Materials: 6 colored hats

Activity: The teacher presents an issue and asks students to reply using a particular thinking hat.

Red hat: Feelings.   What are my feelings about this?

Yellow hat: Strengths.   What are the good points?

Black hat: Weaknesses. What is wrong with this?

Green hat: New ideas.   What is possible?

White hat: Information. What are the facts?

Blue hat: Thinking about thinking. What thinking is needed?

Example:

All students should wear school uniforms. Teacher: Put on your yellow hat and tell me the good points.

The military draft is being reinstated.

All U.S. citizens will be required to vote in every city, state, and federal election.

Stem cell research – is it ethical?

Your city has passed an ordinance that requires all residents to recycle.

What if there were no schools?

More Topics for Six Thinking Hats: Nose rings, piercing body parts, censorship, pesticides, migration, immigration, affirmative action, space exploration, famous people, mobile phones, cheerleaders, zoos, Thanksgiving dinner.

69. SONGSTER

Intro: Music and rhythm activities help embed learning (like the alphabet song), energize or calm students, as well as increase student attentiveness.

Brain Link	Brain Processing Preference	Content Skill	Thinking Skill
Novelty Challenge Social interaction Humor	Musical/ Rhythmic Verbal/Linguistic Auditory Analytic Individual, pairs or groups	All	Synthesis Composing Originality Organizing skills Risk taking Sequencing Memorizing

Materials: paper and pencil

Brain Song: The more students understand about their brains, the more they can comprehend the concept of learning. Teach them the parts of the brain by using the tune of *Ten Little Indians*. Students will use two hands to point to each area of the brain as they sing:

♦ Frontal, temporal, occipital, parietal (3 times)
♦ Cerebellum, brainstem

    <u>Areas to point to</u>:

        Frontal (forehead)
        Temporal (temples)
        Occipital (back of head)
        Parietal (top of head)
        Cerebellum (lower back of head below the bump)
        Brain stem (top of neck)

Activity: Students use a tune they already know and write a song on a specific aspect of a theme, and then perform it for the class.

Possible songs to songster with:

Old MacDonald	Row, Row, Row Your Boat
Mary Had a Little Lamb	Twinkle, Twinkle Little Star
London Bridges	Three Blind Mice
Are you Sleeping?	Itsy Bitsy Spider
My Bonnie Lies over the Ocean	The Twelve Days of Christmas
Yankee Doodle	Jingle Bells
She'll be Comin' Round the Mountain	Bingo

70. SOUND EFFECTS STORY

<u>Intro</u>: This activity keeps the attention of the whole class. Students will actively listen and participate.

Brain Link	Brain Processing Preference	Content Skill	Thinking Skill
Novelty Pattern seeking Challenge Social interaction Humor	Verbal/ Linguistic Interpersonal Analytic Auditory Individual Pairs	Comprehension Fluency Sequence Listening	Organizing skills Analysis Imagination Risk taking

<u>Materials</u>: Vocabulary or story words; example of a sound effects story

<u>Activity</u>:   Students write stories and assign sound effects for certain words. The class is divided into sections and given a word with a sound effect to repeat each time the storyteller speaks their word.

<u>Example</u>:
Monsters: THUMP! THUMP! THUMP!   Victim: HELP! HELP! HELP!
Mummies: OO-AH! OO-AH! OO-AH!   Midnight: Dong 12 times

Once upon a time, there was a trillion year old <u>Mummy</u> (OO-AH! OO-AH! OO-AH!) who was afraid of <u>Monsters</u> (THUMP! THUMP! THUMP!). The <u>Mummy</u> (OO-AH! OO-AH! OO-AH!) had been a VICTIM (HELP! HELP! HELP!) of cruel Leprechauns in ancient times.

71. SPELLATHON

Intro: Students are totally engaged in this activity and love to compete for the highest score.

Brain Link	Brain Processing Preference	Content Skill	Thinking Skill
Attention/Focus Practice Activate prior knowledge Challenge	Verbal/Linguistic Analytic Tactile	Spelling Vocabulary	Analysis Problem solving

Materials: paper, pencil and copy of Spellathon below (Optional: dictionary)

Activity: Students spell as many 4-letter and 5-letter words by moving along the connected lines from one letter to another in the diagram. Do not skip any letters. You may come back to a letter and use it twice in the same word (briar), but do not stay on a letter, using it twice (bull). To make it more challenging no words beginning with a capital letter or ending in plural "s" are allowed; no foreign words are allowed. Count 2 points for each 4-letter word and 4 points for each 5-letter word.

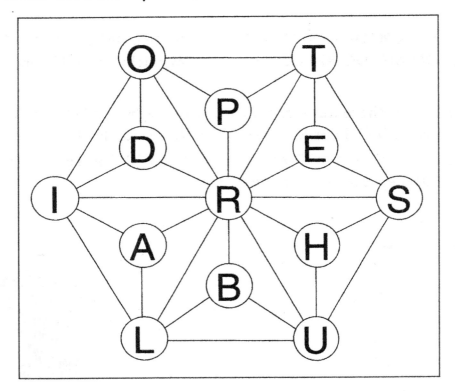

72. SYNONYMS AND ANTONYMS

Intro: Do you get tired of your students using the same tired old words? The activity is a way to encourage your students to think about alternative words choices.

Brain Link	Brain Processing Preference	Content Skill	Thinking Skill
Trigger emotions Challenge Novelty Mind body link	Verbal/Linguistic Interpersonal Individual, pairs or groups	Comprehension Synonyms Antonyms Rhyming Language development Word study Vocabulary	Comprehension Flexibility Analysis Risk taking Attributes

Materials: A list of synonyms and antonyms. Group the words into three and be sure to have the synonym or antonym answers rhyme.

Activity: Divide students into teams or four. Each pair acts out the words given and the other pair must guess the actions and find an alternative word. All three words will rhyme.

Synonym examples: Locomotive, wheat, trail = train, grain, and lane

stroll	conversation	stare
harvest	beverage	policeman
sightless	tie	good
lament	ripped	hatched

(walk, talk, gawk; crop, pop, cop; blind, bind, kind; mourn, torn, born)

Antonym examples: white, front, plenty = black, back, lack

rise	start	bottom
enemy	borrow	beginning
loose	blindness	left
repair	give	genuine

(drop, stop, top; friend, lend, end; tight, sight, right; break, take, fake)

73. $10,000 PYRAMID

Intro: This activity is exciting and a great way to review vocabulary. It is similar to the T.V. show, $10,000 Pyramid and can be used for any content.

Brain Link	Brain Processing Preference	Content Skill	Thinking Skill
Novelty Challenge Social interaction Humor	Verbal/Linguistic Interpersonal Auditory Partner	Vocabulary Listening	Fluency Risk taking Attributes

Materials: Handout or transparency of categories

Activity: Students pair up and sit facing one another. Partner A will give the clues while partner B tries to guess the answers. The teacher calls out the category, and Partner A gives clues describing the word. Any word can be skipped and revisited by saying, "Pass." Partners change roles after 3-4 rounds.

To make the game more challenging:

♦ Reduce the time from 45 seconds per category to 35 then to 20 seconds.

♦ Do not let students use their hands to help describe the words.

Example: "This vegetable is orange and Bugs Bunny likes to eat it."

Vegetables	Parts of Speech	Pets/Animals	Geometry	Zoo Animals
Carrots	Adjective	Cat	Square	Lion
Onions	Noun	Dog	Rectangle	Bear
Celery	Adverb	Hamster	Circle	Elephant
Corn	Verb	Bird	Triangle	Seal
Potatoes	Pronoun	Fish	Radius	Giraffe
Green beans	Conjunction	Snake	Perimeter	Alligator
Lettuce	Preposition	Mouse	Circumference	Monkey

74. THE LETTER IS A...

<u>Intro</u>:   Spice up vocabulary terms by creating word lists that begin with the same letter.

Brain Link	Brain Processing Preference	Content Skill	Thinking Skill
Challenge Novelty Pattern seeking	Verbal/Linguistic Analytic Individual	All	Problem solving Flexibility

<u>Materials</u>: content related words, paper and pencil

<u>Activity</u>:
<u>Theme: Language</u>   Answers

A word that indicates how, when or where   _____   adverb

Form of *a* used before vowel sounds   _____   an

To shorten   _____   abbreviate

Occurrence of same sound at the
   beginning of several words   _____   alliteration

Describing word   _____   adjective

A palatial likeness between things that
   are compared   _____   analogy

Story in which the characters end events
   symbolize some deeper underlying meaning   _____   allegory

Short amusing story about a real person
   or event   _____   anecdote

To add notes of explanation   _____   annotate

Sign used to show that letters have
   been omitted   _____   apostrophe

The writer of a book   _____   author

75. 30 (OR 50) WORD SUMMARY

Intro: This strategy is a twist on the written "report." It serves to reinforce, clarify, and summarize key points of class lessons or text material.

Brain Link	Brain Processing Preference	Content Skill	Thinking Skill
Challenge Practice	Verbal/Linguistic Analytic Individual, pairs, groups	Summarizations	Analysis Originality Summarizing

Materials: paper and pencil

Activity:
Students identify key concepts and words that were presented in a lesson. These ideas should be used to write a thirty-word summary of the lesson or a specific part of the lesson.

76. THROW THE DICE

Intro: This hands-on review strategy is like a game.

Brain Link	Brain Processing Preference	Content Skill	Thinking Skill
Social interaction Reflection Practice	Verbal/Linguistic Tactile Analytic Groups	All	Comprehension Elaboration Analysis

Materials: dice, teacher-made questions

Activity:
Divide students into groups of 4 to 6. Each group has a die and a question sheet. A student rolls the die, and that is the question number that he or she must answer. You can use two dice and 9 or 10 questions. This gives students a lucky roll to pass.

Example: Novel
1. What were the major strengths and weaknesses of the protagonist in this story?
2. What were the major strengths and weaknesses of the antagonist in this story?
3. Describe the setting of the story.
4. What was the major conflict in the story and how was it resolved?
5. What was the point of view used to tell the story?
6. On a scale of 1 to 10, give your ranking of the story. Explain your answer.

77. TOP TEN LISTS

Intro: Adding humor to routine practice is motivating and fun for your students. This activity allows for imagination and creativity.

Brain Link	Brain Processing Preference	Content Skill	Thinking Skill
Challenge Practice Humor Novelty	Verbal/Linguistic Analytic Individual, pairs, groups	Following directions Comprehension Summarizations Word meaning	Problem solving Analysis Fluency Flexibility Attributes Risk taking Imagination

Materials: paper and pencil

Activity: Students create a Top Ten List related to their current unit of study.

Top Ten Signs That You are at a Bad Zoo.
    10. The stripes on the zebra tend to peel away in the heat.
    9. The Lion in the lion cage closely resembles the one from The Lion King.

More ideas!
Top Ten Reasons to Give Blood
Top Ten Useless Inventions
Top Ten Reasons Why Exercise is Good
Top Ten Mistakes made by Explorers
Top Ten Most Often Misspelled Words
Top Ten Things Kids Learn While Surfing the Internet
Top Ten Homework Excuses
Top Ten Things All Parents Should Know about Kids
Top Ten Most Commonly Used Slang Terms by Kids
Top Ten Reasons for *Not* Watching Television

78. TOSS THE BALL

Intro: Reviewing material makes learning more fun when tossing a ball.

Brain Link	Brain Processing Preference	Content Skill	Thinking Skill
Challenge Practice Multiple memory pathways	Verbal/Linguistic Interpersonal Analytic Groups	All	Risk taking Flexibility Problem solving

Materials: koosh ball or soft squeeze ball for tossing

Activity: Students stand in a circle and toss a sponge ball to one another after answering and then asking a question.

Students start with a question, look at a person, ask them the question completely, and then toss the ball. The person who receives the ball answers the question and then continues by asking another question.
Remind students
- to first make eye contact.
- to ask the question completely.
- to gently toss the ball underhanded so that it arches high in the air and no higher than shoulders.

Examples: Students can ask for personal information such as name, birthday, number of brothers and sisters, pets

Topic: Grammar
- Name two prepositions.
- What is a conjunction's function?

Topic: Math
- What is 5 times 6?
- What is 9 divided by 3?
- What is the square root of 9?

79. TRIANGLE LISTENING INTERVIEWS

Intro: Many students need to work on critical listening skills. This activity teaches them to tune in and interpret what they hear.

Brain Link	Brain Processing Preference	Content Skill	Thinking Skill
Trigger emotions Social interaction Feedback Reflection and evaluation	Interpersonal Verbal/Linguistic Analytic Auditory Groups of 3	Summarizing Listening Paraphrasing	Analysis Observe Point of view

Materials: none

Activity: Students work in groups of three and discuss an idea or issue related to a specific theme.
- Listener
- Talker
- Observer

1. The talker talks for one minute answering a question or giving opinions.

2. The listener gives a summary of the main points.

5. The observer makes brief comments about whether or not he/she thinks the listener's summary was accurate.

6. Everyone moves to the next chair and the activity is repeated.

80. TURNABOUTS

__Intro__: Some words can be turned around to spell a different word.

Brain Link	Brain Processing Preference	Content Skill	Thinking Skill
Attention/Focus Practice Feedback Activate prior knowledge Novelty	Verbal/Linguistic Analytic Individual, small groups	Vocabulary Spelling Dictionary skills Following directions	Brainstorming Fluency Flexibility Risk taking Analysis

__Materials__: paper and pencil

__Activity__: Have students brainstorm or find words that follow the rule.
Examples:

NUTS	to STUN
NET	to TEN
BAT	to TAB
BRAG	to BRAG
TON	to NOT

81. 20 QUESTIONS

Intro: Working in a team can be challenging. This activity keeps all team members focused and actively engaged.

Brain Link	Brain Processing Preference	Content Skill	Thinking Skill
Novelty Challenge Social interaction	Verbal/Linguistic Interpersonal Analytic Auditory Small groups	All	Attributes Analysis, Classify Cause/Effect Decision making Evaluation Inferring, Predicting Sequencing

Materials: paper pencil

Activity: Divide the class into groups of four or five. Using your theme or topic, tell students that their group will be asking questions that can only be answered with "yes" or "no." Students work together to decide on the order to ask the questions. This forces students to think in a fashion of "if . . .then . . ." If the answer is no, then we do not need to ask questions that deal with that aspect. One team will ask the questions of the teacher. The other teams will listen and try to figure out the answer. If one of those teams thinks they have the answer, a team member must write it down, and bring the paper to the teacher. The teacher will not respond to the answers by other teams until the questioning team has an answer or asked their 20 questions.
Points can be awarded to the teams with the correct answer.

Example: The teacher tells the students that the answer is an accessory and related to our unit on weather. (The answer could be anything from galoshes to flip flops, an umbrella, sweater, ski goggles, etc.)

Variation: Create a list of words connected to a theme or topic. Divide students into teams. Each team studies the words. The teacher secretly chooses one word from the list, and the groups compete to guess what the word is. The questioning group should only ask "Yes" or "No" questions. Questions should be asked about structure, not the meaning of the word. For example: Is it before the letter L in the alphabet? Is it a proper noun? Is it a plural? Does it have 7 letters? Does it have three vowels? Does it have double consonants? Does it have three syllables?

82. 26 LETTERS MISSING

Intro: This activity looks simple but can be a real challenge! Students will be motivated to complete this activity because it looks easy. Not so! Watch your students as they actively engage in solving this word puzzle.

Brain Link	Brain Processing Preference	Content Skill	Thinking Skill
Challenge Practice Novelty	Verbal/Linguistic Analytic	Word study Vocabulary Spelling Following directions	Analysis

Materials: paper and pencil

Activity: Use content vocabulary or spelling words to write **26 Letters Missing.** Each word will have at least one blank for the student to fill in. There should be 26 blanks. The alphabet letters are used only once. Work through the answers to make sure that each missing letter is used only once. If uncommon letters cannot be used, note it in the directions to your students. "The letter Q and Z will not be used."

Example: Use the 26 letters of the alphabet to complete the words below. Use each letter only once. No foreign words, slang, or contractions allowed.

Topic: Aviation

A B C D E F G H I J K L M N O P Q R S T U V W X Y Z

1. __ L T __ T U __ E
2. __ I F __
3. C O __ K __ I T
4. __ R A __ I T Y
5. __ U S __ L A G E
6. T U R B __ __ E T
7. T __ R __ S T
8. __ I __ G S
9. H __ P O __ I A
10. __ U L U
11. __ A N __
12. __ E __ I D I A N
13. T O R __ U E

Answers: altitude, lift cockpit, gravity, fuselage, turbojet, thrust, wings, hypoxia, Zulu, bank, meridian, torque

83. VENN AGAIN

Intro: Students are asked to find similarities and differences between two things, and present them in a diagram of overlapping circles or ovals.

Differences   Similariities   Differences

Starburst®

Individually
  wrapped
Tub-like
  packaging
Chewy
Fruit flavored

Candy
Different
  colors
Similar cost
Similar size
  packaging
Made by Mars®

M & M®

Not individually
  wrapped
Packaged in a
  bag
Melt in mouth
Chocolate
  flavored

Brain Link	Brain Processing Preference	Content Skill	Thinking Skill
Practice Evaluation Pattern seeking	Logical/Mathematical Visual/Spatial Visual Analytic Individual, pairs or groups	All	Analysis Evaluation Classify Attributes

Materials: paper and pencil

Activity: Students draw a Venn diagram showing a relationship related to class lessons.

Examples:
Make a Venn diagram showing the similarities and differences between Roosevelt and Churchill; Madonna and Brittney Spears; football and soccer; electricity and gas; Harry Potter, Hermione and Ron.

Make a Venn diagram showing the relationships among animals, birds, and ducks, using one circle to represent animals, another for birds, and a third for ducks.

84. WARM UPS = WUPS

Intro: These writing activities help students to structure sentences on sentence length, specific word placement, vocabulary, word function, and internal punctuation in sentences.

Brain Link	Brain Processing Preference	Content Skill	Thinking Skill
Challenge Practice Pattern seeking Rituals	Verbal/Linguistic Analytic Visual Individual	All	Analysis Attributes Brainstorming Fluency Flexibility Originality Elaboration

Materials: Paper and pencil

Activity: Write a sentence using the following letter pattern.

R_____ e_____ a_____ d_____ i_____ n_____ g_____.

P_____ e_____ n_____ c_____ i_____ l_____.

Write a five-word sentence in which the fourth word is pencil.

_____ _____ _____ pencil _____.

Write a six-word sentence in which the second word is pencil.

Write a nine-word sentence in which the first word is pencil.

Write a seven-word sentence in which the second word is **machine** and the fifth word is **pencil**.

Write a sentence using the letters in your name.

L_____ i_____ n_____ d_____ a_____.

J_____ e_____ n_____ n_____ i_____ f_____ e_____ r_____.

Write a sentence in which the first letter of each word is the first letter of the planets as they appear in order from the sun.

M_____ V_____ E_____ M_____ J_____ S_____ U_____ N_____ p_____.

Write a sentence in which the first letter of each word spells the name of a Revolutionary War battle.

S_____ a_____ r_____ a_____ t_____ o_____ g_____ a_____.

Write a sentence in which the initial letters of the words spell the name of
a famous person in history.
W_____ a_____ s_____ h_____ i_____ n_____ g_____ t_____ o_____ n_____.
Write a sentence in which the initial letters of the words spell the name of
an American president.
Write a sentence in which the initial letters of the words spell the name of
a famous person in history.
B_____ i_____ l_____ l_____ c_____ l_____ i_____ n_____ t_____ o_____ n_____.

Write a sentence without using the letter "e."
Write a sentence where nine "T's" appear.
Write a sentence in which each word begins with a vowel.
Write a sentence which ends in an exclamation mark.
Write a sentence that asks a question.
Write a sentence using two of your vocabulary words.
Write as much as you can and as well as you can about Goldilocks. You have
one minute to think before writing and two minutes to write.
Write a sentence that shows great emotion.
Write three related sentences that contain the following ideas: power and
commitment.

Warm Ups for the Outsiders

Write a complete sentence using the following letter pattern.
M_____ a_____ d_____ r_____ a_____ s_____.

Cross out the letter in the word OUTSIDERS that is the second letter
before the middle letter.
Write a nine (9) word sentence in which the 5th word is indignant.
_____ _____ _____ _____ indignant _____ _____ _____ _____.
Write as much as you can as fast as you can about. . . being alone.
Indicate the position of the letter in the word RESEMBLANCE that is 14th
letter in the alphabet.

1. first	5. fifth	9. ninth
2. second	6. sixth	10. tenth
3. third	7. seventh	11. eleventh
4. fourth	8. eighth	

85. WHAT COMES AFTER?

Intro: This activity requires students to see relationships between different words and phrases. It is also a fun way to review compound words.

Brain Link	Brain Processing Preference	Content Skill	Thinking Skill
Novelty Practice Activate prior knowledge	Verbal/Linguistic Analytic Individual Small group	Syllables Word meaning Context clues Spelling	Analysis Classify Find patterns Problem solving Attributes

Materials: paper and pencil

Activity: Students supply a missing word for each set. This activity can be used as a competition. Set a time limit for groups and add up scores.
Example:
Complete the familiar expressions, phrases, or compounds by adding the same word to fill each blank.
Example: measuring _____   silver _____   serving _____
        pay _____   take _____   cast _____
        bare _____   tender _____   under _____
        back _____   under_____   fore_____
        pad _____   inter_____   Goldi_____(s)

Answer: spoon, off, foot, hand, lock

WHAT COMES BEFORE?

Students supply a missing word for each set. This activity can be used as a competition. Set a time limit for groups and add up scores.
Example: ____ cream   _____cube   _____ water
       ____ ware   _____lining   _____ -haired
       ____ rush   _____ finger
       _____ put   _____ grow   _____ let
       _____ coat   _____Sox   _____ handed

Answers: ice, silver, gold, out, red

86. WHAT IF…?

Intro: Students are asked to think about all the possibilities and implications of a hypothetical situation.

Brain Link	Brain Processing Preference	Content Skill	Thinking Skill
Novelty Attention Challenge Relevance Humor Trigger emotions	Verbal/Linguistic Interpersonal Analytic Global Individual Small group	Language	Brainstorming Composing Complexity Curiosity

Materials: Paper and pencil

Activity:

What if Texas was part of Mexico?

What if bees became popular pets?

What if you could change your name?

What if you won $10,000 or one million dollars in the lottery?

What if you woke up one morning and were invisible?

What if your knees would not bend?

What if it rained corn chips?

87. WORD PYRAMID

Intro: Add a twist to reviewing vocabulary meanings and spelling words by using Word Pyramids. This activity forces students to think at a higher level.

Brain Link	Brain Processing Preference	Content Skill	Thinking Skill
Trigger emotions Novelty Practice	Verbal/Linguistic Analytic Visual Individual	Spelling Word study Vocabulary	Flexibility Analysis

Materials: pencil and paper

Activity: Add one letter to each word as you go down.

A
AT
PAT
SPAT
SPLAT

HINTS
NEAR
HAD LUNCH
TARDY
TARDIER
SHAVING CREAM

A
AT
ATE
LATE
LATER
LATHER

LEATHER

88. WORD SCAVENGER HUNT

Intro: Word Scavenger Hunt will make the weekly spelling list much more exciting for your students. Students will categorize a list of spelling words according to word letter structure and meaning.

Brain Link	Brain Processing Preference	Content Skill	Thinking Skill
Novelty Pattern seeking Challenge	Verbal/Linguistic Logical/Mathematical Analytic Tactile/Kinesthetic Individual, pair	Word study Spelling Vocabulary	Attributes Analysis Categorizing Organizing

Materials: Spelling list

Activities:

a. Classify words according to the number of syllables.

b. Classify the nouns on your list. (people, places, things)

c. Classify each word according to the number of letters it contains. Make a bar graph.

d. List the words that have a prefix.

e. List all the words that have a suffix.

f. Give the numerical value for each word. A=1, B=2.....Z=26

g. List all the words that have a double consonant.

h. Classify words according to parts of speech. Color-code any words that fit into more than one category.

i. List the words that are plural.

j. List the words that contain a double vowel.

k. Write the word(s) that has a silent letter.

l. List the words that have long vowel sounds.

m. Write synonyms for five words on the list.

n. Use an adjective to describe each noun on the list.

o. Write each word as many times as it has syllables.

p. Write a rhyming word for as many words as possible.

q. Write your words in Morse Code.

r. Write each word with your finger on a friend's back. Have your friend guess the words.

s. Associate 5 words with people you know or people from history.

t. Give students a Seek and Find puzzle with the spelling words.

89. WRITE IT

Intro: Challenge students to write a paragraph without using a specified letter or word.

Brain Link	Brain Processing Preference	Content Skill	Thinking Skill
Challenge Novelty Practice	Verbal/Linguistic Analytic Individual	Sequence Punctuation Grammar Word study	Imagination Elaboration Originality Analysis Synthesis

Materials: paper and pencil

Activity:
Write a sentence or a paragraph using no Es. Now try a paragraph.

An Odd Paragraph

You probably cannot find any paragraph in a journal that is as unusual as this paragraph. But what is odd about it? That is hard to say at first, but as you study it, you will catch on, no doubt. I will add that you might look through thousands of paragraphs in *any* book or journal - all containing as many words as this - and not find any that can boast this oddity. Do you know what it is?

(no letter E)

90. WUZZLES

Intro: Wuzzles are a combination of words, pictures, or symbols that exercise both sides of the brain simultaneously.

Brain Link	Brain Processing Preference	Content Skill	Thinking Skill
Humor Novelty Challenge Pattern seeking	Logical/Mathematical Visual/Spatial Verbal/Linguistic Interpersonal	All	Analysis Synthesis Brainstorming Complexity Problem solving

Materials: Wuzzles

Activity: To solve the Wuzzles you must try to discover the familiar word, phrase, saying or name represented by each arrangement of letters, pictures, or symbols in the boxes.
For example, MEEATINGALS would represent "eating between meals."
Design Wuzzles around a theme or topic or have students create their own.

Topic: Language Arts

THE PL**OT**	R/E/A/D/I/N/G	**1T3456**	ABCDEFGH^{I}JKLM NOP^{Q}RSTUVWXYZ
EILNPU	ONCE 5 PM	MD MD	HAMLET WORDS
1 at 3:46	NOXQQIVIT	Word YYY	No ways it ways

Answers: the plot thickens, reading between the lines, tea for two, high IQ, line up in alphabetical order, once upon a time, paradox, a play on words, one at a time, no excuse for it, word wise, no two ways about it.

GLOSSARY

Activating prior knowledge: recalling something learned previously relative to the topic or task

Analogy: a comparison showing similar relationships

Analyzing skills: core-thinking skills that involve clarifying information by examining parts and relationships

Analysis: breaking into parts to determine meaning; taking apart, identifying elements, relationships

Attention: conscious control of mental focus on particular information

Attribute recognition: the ability to assign a name or label to the common features within a set of information

Bias: a one-sided or slanted point of view

Brainstorming: an idea-generating strategy often used for team problem solving

Compare/Contrast: identify similarities and differences

Classify/Sort: grouping, ordering, or organizing items or concepts based on characteristics, uses, or relationships

Cause and Effect: recognizing actions and their reactions

Composing: the process of developing a composition, which may be written, musical, mechanical, or artistic

Comprehending: generating meaning or understanding

Complexity: a skill that enables the learner to create structure in an unstructured setting or to bring a logical order to a given situation

Curiosity: a skill that enables the learner to follow a hunch, question alternatives, ponder outcomes, and wonder about options in a given situation

Curriculum: a structured series of intended learning outcomes

Decision-making: selecting from among alternatives

Elaboration: adding details, explanations, examples, or other relevant information from prior knowledge

Evaluation: judging using criteria

Encoding skills: remembering skills that involve storing information in long-term memory

Establishing criteria: setting standards for making judgments

Evaluating skills: core thinking skills that involve assessing the reasonableness and quality of ideas

Fact and Opinion: fact - that which can be proved or disproved; opinion - a belief or judgment

Find Patterns: detecting repetitions

Fluency: a skill that enables the learner to generate lots of ideas, oodles of related answers, scads of operations, or a heap of choices in a given situation

Flexibility a skill that enables the learner to change everyday objects to fit a variety of categories by taking detours and varying size, shape, quantities, time limits, requirements, objectives, or dimensions in a given situation

Focusing skills: core-thinking skills that involve selected pieces of information and ignoring others

Identifying attributes and components: determining characteristics or parts of something

Identifying relationships and patterns: recognizing ways elements are related

Imagination: a skill that enables the learner to visualize possibilities, build images in one's mind, picture new objects, or reach beyond the limits of the practical in response to a given situation

Inferring: going beyond available information to identify what may reasonably be true; deriving meaning from cues, hints, evidence

Integrating skills: core skills that involve connecting or combining information

Metacognition: a dimension of thinking that involves knowledge and control of self and knowledge and control of process

Mnemonics: a set of encoding strategies that involve linking bits of information together through visual or semantic connections

Observe: use one or more of the senses to increase one's perception and gather information; using your senses to learn about something in detail

Originality: a skill that enables the learner to seek the unusual or not obvious by suggesting clever twists to change content or arrive at strategies to seek the novel in a given situation

Organizing skills: core-thinking skills that involve arranging information so that it can be used more effectively

Planning: developing strategies to reach a specific goal; delineation of end-means relationships

Point of View: determining perspectives

Predicting: determining what will happen next

Problem solving: analyzing a perplexing or difficult situation for the purpose of generating a solution

Ranking: a rating system that forces prioritization of choices

Recalling skills: remembering skills that involve retrieving information from long-term memory

Rehearsal: an encoding strategy that involves repeated processing of information

Remembering skills: core thinking skills that involve conscious efforts to store and retrieve information.

Retrieval: accessing previously encoded information

Risk Taking: a skill that enables the learner to deal with the unknown by taking chances, experimenting with new ideas, or trying new challenges in a given situation

Setting goals: a focusing skill that involves establishing direction and purpose

Sequencing: arranging things in an order

Summarizing: restate in a simplified or condensed version

HAND HOPPER PUZZLE

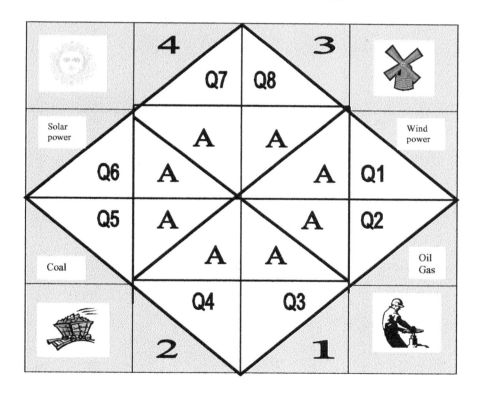

CUBE IT PATTERN

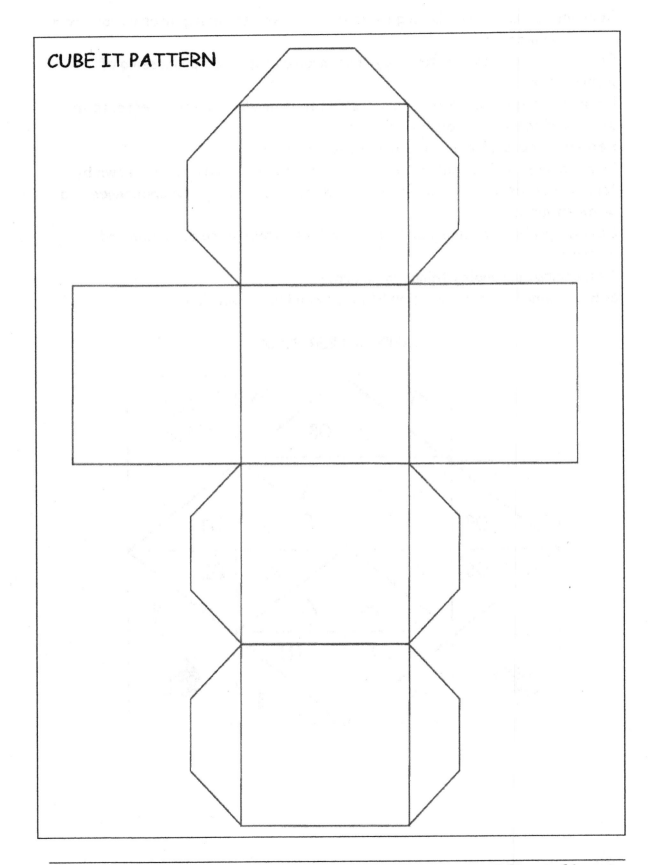

COMPOUND WORDS

Airplane
Applesauce
Armrest
Bedbug
Blackboard
Bluebird
Bookmark
Borderline
Briefcase
Buttonhole
Candlelight
Cardboard
Cherrystone
Compounds
Countdown
Courthouse
Cowboy
Crabgrass
Doghouse
Fairway
Fingernail
Fingerprint
Fingertip
Fireside
Flowerpot
Footprint
Funhouse
Girlfriend
Grapefruit
Grapevine
Greenhouse
Guideline

Gunrunner
Handshake
Headache
Homebody
Homecoming
Homemade
Honeycomb
Honeymoon
Honeysuckle
Hotshot
Kingpin
Ladylike
Landscape
Lawnmower
Letterhead
Mainstream
Milkman
Motorboat
Needlepoint
Paperweight
Piecemeal
Pigeonhole
Pigskin
Playbill
Printout
Railroad
Raincoat
Rattlesnake
Restroom
Roommate
Shadowbox

Sharecropper
Sheepskin
Sidekick
Slowdown
Somehow
Someone
Sometime
Springboard
Stagecoach
Staircase
Steamship
Storehouse
Stovepipe
Stowaway
Strawberry
Strongbox
Sunburn
Sunglasses
Sunshine
Supernatural
Tablecloth
Threadbare
Timekeeper
Toothbrush
Wallpaper
Washcloth
Wastepaper
Watermelon
Waterproof
Whitewash
Wristwatch

WORD PENTAGON

Art	Bear	Par	Tap
At	Beat	Part	Tar
Ate	Beet	Pat	Tarp
Babe	Bet	Rap	Tart
Bar	Ear	Rat	Tea
Bat	Eat	Rate	Tear
Be	Papa	Tab	trap

PALINDROMES

Words that are spelled the same forward and backward. Example: rotor

1. A time of day.	noon
2. Baby's dinner garment.	bib
3. A young dog	pup
4. A boy's name	bob
5. Another name for father	pop
6. What you need at a rally	pep
7. A little child	
8. A form, of "do"	did
9. The first woman	eve
10. Allows us to see	eye
11. The sound a bird makes	peep
12. Document showing ownership of land	deed
13. A joke	gag
14. Female religious person	nun
15. Instrument for detecting airplanes	radar
16. The sound made by a horn	toot
17. An Eskimo boat	kayak
18. Carpenter's instrument with a bubble in it	level
19. A polite title for a lady	madam